The question "What is my calling?" burns in the hea... ...s
addressed this question with powerful answers in he... ...n
discovering your passion at the start of your journey, ...as
you asking God, "What's next?"—this book is for you!"

—*David and Nicole Binion*
Pastors, Dwell Church, Dallas, Texas

Polls indicate the hunger to find one's purpose is the strongest desire motivating most of us. After many detours and much frustration, I found mine—and in so doing, I found myself. With this wonderful book by Jen Tringale, your journey to self-identity and fulfillment can avoid many needless delays and pitfalls. I wish I'd have had it early in my journey!

—*Dutch Sheets*
Dutch Sheets Ministries, Cold Springs, Colorado

Most people know that there is a purpose for their life. The problem is that they do not know how to align their life with that purpose. Jen Tringale will help you create your own path, leading you to the place of discovering your personal purpose and fulfilling your destiny.

—*Roberts Liardon*
Author, God's Generals series
Founder, Roberts Liardon Ministries, Embassy International Church

Jen Tringale's message empowers believers to walk in the fullness of God's calling and see the glory of God impact this generation. Many aspects of growing into your calling are covered in this book in a practical, but deeply spiritual, way. It is provoking, challenging, and inspiring, all the while pointing us to Jesus.

—*Patsy Cameneti*
Senior Pastor, Rhema Family Church, Rhema Bible College, Brisbane, Australia

Wow! Jen Tringale has written an incredible book that will put you on the right path to fulfilling your calling! You'll find faith-filled encouragement to discover the call of God on your life. This is a must-read for anyone who desires to fulfill their destiny and the dream God has placed in their heart.

—*Beth Jones*
Pastor, Valley Family Church, Kalamazoo, Michigan / TV host, *The Basics with Beth*

A well-thought-out, easy-to-understand work that allows you to embark on the journey of answering the questions "Why am I here?" and "What am I to do?" Jen doesn't just lead you on the path; she also equips you with the tools to find the answer.

—*Sara Conner*
Pastor, Word of Truth Family Church, Arlington, TX

Jen Tringale delivers powerful inspiration and profound insights to guide you into aligning your pursuits according to the trajectory of your destiny. Prepare to find your place, get into position, and take up your calling to walk out a destiny that's brighter and more beautiful than anything you have ever dared to imagine!

—*Dr. Pat Hagin-Harrison*
President and founder, Faith Christian Fellowship International, Tulsa, Oklahoma

The riches penned on these pages could well be the greatest game-changer yet for the person with an open heart and a willingness to leave the fear-dependent safe harbor of comfortable predictability. Jen Tringale makes it crystal clear: you were designed to push outward—to explore, discover, lead and enrich the world around you. Unfurl your sails, and let them fill with the divine winds of your *Calling*!

—*Len and Cathy Mink*
Len Mink Ministries, Tulsa, Oklahoma

Jen Tringale not only discerns the season of God in the earth, but she also navigationally challenges the reader into discerning the rhythms of the DNA of their own destinies. This book is a powerful, inspiring, and practical work for any believer who desires to discover, develop, and deploy their purpose and calling.

—*Reverends Cookie and Fred Brothers*
Faith Christian Fellowship International, Tulsa, Oklahoma

If you are tired of the status quo and ready to challenge life as usual, this book will serve as a gateway into your destined place and help you to recognize that you are right on time! Let this book propel you into your right-now appointed time and moment.

—*Dr. Mary Frances Varallo*
President, Mary Frances Varallo Ministries, Nashville, Tennessee

The perfect book to help you discover your unique calling and gain understanding for the journey to fulfilling your destiny. Deeply inspiring and perfectly practical, it is a must-read for anyone passionate about pursuing Jesus and the extraordinary plans God has for them.

—*Nicole Smithee*
CEO and founder, Iridescent, New York, New York

Jen Tringale's new book gives people the answers they are so desperately searching for. Through Jen's insights and personal stories, she creates a beautiful and easy-to-understand road map of answers for so many of life's questions. *Calling* will bring clarity to anyone regarding their destiny and a deeper understanding of the greater purpose for their life.

—*Chad and Marla Rowe*
Pastors, Destiny World Outreach Center, Killeen, Texas

CALLING

UNDERSTANDING YOUR
PURPOSE, PLACE & POSITION

JEN TRINGALE

INTERNATIONAL AUTHOR AND SPEAKER

WHITAKER
HOUSE

CALLING
Understanding Your Purpose, Place & Position

Jen Tringale
jentringale.com
Jen Tringale Ministries
P.O. Box 161205
Ft. Worth, TX 76161

ISBN: 978-1-64123-146-6
eBook ISBN: 978-1-64123-147-3
Printed in the United States of America
© 2018 by Jen Tringale

Whitaker House
1030 Hunt Valley Circle
New Kensington, PA 15068
www.whitakerhouse.com

Library of Congress Cataloging-in-Publication Data
Names: Tringale, Jen, 1977– author.
Title: Calling : understanding your purpose, place & position / Jen Tringale.
Description: New Kensington, PA : Whitaker House, 2018. |
Identifiers: LCCN 2018025503 (print) | LCCN 2018030006 (ebook) | ISBN 9781641231473 (e-book) | ISBN 9781641231466 (alk. paper)
Subjects: LCSH: Vocation—Christianity.
Classification: LCC BV4740 (ebook) | LCC BV4740 .T75 2018 (print) | DDC 248.4—dc23
LC record available at https://lccn.loc.gov/2018025503

1 2 3 4 5 6 7 8 9 10 11 ⨇ 25 24 23 22 21 20 19 18

Contents

Foreword

The journey of life is an odyssey as we seek out meaning, purpose, and destiny. Questions arise from thoughtful hearts in strategic moments: Why am I here? What was I born to do? Who am I? Thankfully, God wants us to have the answers, and the insight Jen shares in this book help us to gain clarity and understanding for our individual lives. They are life-changing principles that will open up to us futures of hope and fulfillment.

The cry for significance is answered in amazing truths revealed throughout the Word. God thinks about you. The brilliant Creator of the heavens and earth, who meticulously designed the universe, thinks about you; His thoughts about you are continuously good. The apostle Paul told his son in the faith, Timothy, that God had called him and given him purpose before time began. (See 2 Timothy 1:9.) The original word Paul used for "purpose" is filled with meaning. It is the word *prosthesis*; *pro* means "before," and *thesis* is a written report, composition, or essay. Ponder this: Paul says way back in the eternity past, before time began, the Godhead thought about why you would be, why you would exist. The prophet Jeremiah tells us they thought through plans for you. They wrote a composition with your name on it. Then God created you with gifts, talents, and abilities you would need to fulfill those intentions, meaning that your life has spent time in the awesome mind of God. The Father, Son, and Holy Spirit have plans for you. You are loved and you are significant. This book will help you understand that. It will help you define your purpose, your worth, and destiny will be revealed. And perhaps most importantly, it will give you instruction to help you live it out.

I have watched Jen live the principles she writes about. She was part of our student ministries and later I became her pastor for many years. Eventually, she joined our pastoral staff. We were able to truly know her and have been privileged to watch her as an outstanding woman of God, a champion of our faith, and a leader with a clear message of faith and hope. She is a gifted minister, teacher, and an author writing life truths that inspire, challenge, and instruct. We are so proud of her!

I love the Hebrew concept of destiny and purpose. It admonishes to never give up on your future, no matter what obstacles come your way. It clearly declares God will never give up on you. In Jeremiah 29:11, God promised to give us *"an expected end"* (KJV). The word "end" in the Hebrew language is *archariyth*, meaning "out on the horizon." God has purpose out on the horizon for you. It is also the word used to describe rowing a boat. If you've ever been in a rowboat, you know that often, you paddle it backwards. The front of the boat is before you and you lean into the oars going backwards. What a picture Father God paints for us! When you can see where you've been, but can't see over your shoulder clearly where you are going, just keep rowing. God says, "I see the way and I have a plan. When you are rowing hard and your destiny is a speck on the horizon, just keep rowing. When you are rowing by faith and not by sight, don't stop. I've got purpose for you. Listen to My voice calling you out to new horizons and row into your future with Me."

Now, sit back and enjoy as Jen teaches you how to understand your purpose, place, and position. Take to heart God "calling" in this awesome revelation.

—*Dr. Tim Sheets*
Apostle and author, Tim Sheets Ministries

PREFACE

I am forever grateful for the faithfulness of God for downloading this book to my heart and giving me the ability to articulate what needed to be said. Days and nights of writing in between ministry trips on the road were a real-life reminder that God's Word really is our heart's energy, our *daily* bread. This book was written through a particularly tough season in the very beginning of the year. Through this journey, I was reminded that the most important assignments along your path typically come with a "war at the gates." The enemy of your soul sets up like an arsonist of purpose at the threshold of all you are called to affect in an attempt to burn up your passion, vision, and hope. But through this journey, I was freshly reminded of two things. First, that Jesus is "the call" we are all called to. He is so very personal and wonderful and He is the supreme strategic investor. He finds ways to bring benefit out of everything we allow Him to touch and He turns it into gold—something of great value.

Secondly, the kingdom of God has a strategy for momentum. I see it as something like this: the greater your dependency on God, the more movement takes place. Your power is in daily identifying your singular *Savior*, Jesus, and letting go of any stand-ins or imposters, including your own self-sufficiency. You and God working together is what moves you through the gate and into your new place. My hope is that as you read this book, you will find your heart full and more deeply satisfied than when you began, and your faith emboldened. A loved person is a bold person.

"For whoever desires to save his life will lose it, but whoever loses his life for My sake will find it." (Matthew 16:25)

"Arise O Prophet! Work My will,
Thou that hast now perceived and heard.
On land and sea thy charge fulfill
And burn Man's heart with this My Word."
—*Dr. Alexander Pushkin*

ACKNOWLEDGMENTS

Thank you to my parents, Robert and Jean Tringale, for raising me to value the instinct to listen to my heart. Thank you to my publisher, Whitaker House, to Christine Whitaker, and staff for your patience and belief in the power of this book. Thank you to Don Milam at Whitaker House, who always seemed to call at just the right time with the right words to keep going. To Peg Fallon for your great efforts in editing and keeping this project moving forward amidst my crazy travel schedule! Thank you to Rosa Reed for insisting that I write Chapter 5 and for standing beautifully in the unique calling on your life. To Jean Tringale for letting me bounce page after page off of you at all hours of the day and night and for your sage wisdom to "just walk away from it for a few minutes." :) To Dr. Mary Frances Varallo for your encouragement through this process. You have been both a proclaimer and equipper in my life and I am forever grateful. To Kaira (pronounced *Care-Ra*; you're welcome) McKinnon, for keeping everything running so I could steal away to write! The depth of your heart and talent pool never cease to amaze me! Thank you to my pastors, Chad and Marla Rowe, and my Destiny World Outreach family for your constant love, prayer, and support. Thank you to Fred and Cookie Brothers and the FCF Family for being a driving force committed to innovation in this generation; your support and encouragement has been a great supply!

Thank you to my prayer team that prays for me every week out on the road. I can't thank you enough for what you do behind the scenes in making the way. Thank you to our Partners, the best in the world, who have stood in faith, love, and financial partnership, and contributed to reaching people and awakening destiny all around the world!

For this book, I would like to specifically thank the people in my life who were among the "first" to exemplify and teach me the realities of God.

First, Pastor Jim and Jennifer Peterson, two individuals who have fanned the flame of the call of God in tens of thousands of young people, including me. Thank you for your sacrifice and dedication to see and develop the gifts in others. You stand among the greats for all you are and all you have sown. Your church and ministry continue to be a well of refreshing, strength, and prophetic inspiration that I can come back to.

To Pastor Cleddie and Gaynell Keith, growing up at your church in the early years of my life holds some of my greatest childhood memories. What your pastoral care has meant to my family through the years is worth more than gold. Thank you for being the caliber of ministers that you have always been. I respect you greatly.

To Dr. Mike and Colleen Murray, your example of ministry has always been one I hold close. Watching not just what you did but how you did it and your unending supply of love for people made a great impression on me. Your standard of excellence in ministry has always informed my vision. Thank you for being the superb pastors and leaders that you are.

To Dr. Tim and Carol Sheets, thank you for seeing something in me from the start and for creating space for me to use my voice on the platform you have sown your lives to establish. Thank you for exemplifying to me the power of true commitment and loyalty and for setting the example of multi-generational leadership.

To Len and Cathy Mink, in so many ways you were my "Masters Class" in the ministry and you set the bar on excellence. Thank you for loving me like your "other daughter" and for constantly showing me how to take the high road in life. You are two of the most generous people I know. Your ministry has changed my life in ways I can't even describe and the connection we share is one I treasure most. I love you both very much.

To my Rhema family, Rhema is in many ways the house that built me. It is where God directed me to go to be equipped. It was a beginning place for me to join the ranks and march around the world with this mandate we carry. It is an honor to run with each one of you.

Finally, thank you to all of the women that influenced me who walk in their own calling confidently, without excuse or apology. Your life allowed me to see the possibility of what God could do with me and emboldened my "yes." From my heart, thank you to my grandmother, Billie Mae Burkart; my mother, Jean Tringale; my aunt, Pastor Jennifer Peterson; Rev. Leigh Ann Merrell Soesbee; Rev. Cathy Mink; Dr. Mary Frances Varallo; Dr. Pat Hagin-Harrison; Pastor Karen Mosely; Rev. Helen Williams; Trish Hodge; Rev. Patsy Cameneti; and Gloria Copeland.

INTRODUCTION

A new landscape is emerging. Mainstream sociologists are declaring, "We aren't living in a normal moment."

How in the face of a changing world does one train an instinct for affecting what is going on? Even analysts are asking, "How do you train an instinct that knows how to reach a world that is operating in a completely new way to human history? How do you develop an instinct to handle the inheritance of the last generation's vision, buildings, protocols, and inventions? What do you do when you are confronted with what you have never experienced—perhaps never even considered?"

The answer is that you rely totally on the word of God, and the instincts coming from the Spirit of God within you. Every day becomes a series of circumstances for which there is no rational answer, only an instinctive response.

People can continue to believe that our current ways of doing things will work out just fine—that our leadership models will right themselves eventually—but there is a moment ahead for all of us. For some, it will be amazing. For others, crushing. But for everyone, it will be a moment in which things will happen that none of our old ideas, protocols, or senses will help us understand.

The ones who will hear the key change in the music of our culture are the ones who will lead in it, influence it, and have success in it. These are the ones who will learn instinctively how to see potential, and know how to unlock it through their *Calling*. This is the new era requirement of the called in this generation: to do what Jesus did in the midst of the thick, hazy storm of culture in Galilee—get right in the middle of it, and be a revolutionary.

—*Jen Tringale*

"I don't want any messages saying 'I'm holding my position.'... Our plan of operation is to advance and keep on advancing."
—U.S. Army General George S. Patton

CHAPTER 1

YOUR CALLING, YOUR DESTINY

She was just a little girl from White Sulphur Springs, West Virginia, who loved to count things. The daughter of a farmer and a teacher, she counted everything. The steps to the road, the steps up to church, the number of dishes and silverware she washed—anything that could be counted. And so it began for this young, African-American girl from West Virginia, born in 1918.

A day would come when the world paused while she calculated the trajectory for putting the first United States astronaut into space.[1]

On February 20, 1962, John Glenn became the first U.S. astronaut to orbit earth—a monumental moment for the country. The Academy Award-winning movie, *Hidden Figures*[2], highlights how Glenn, uneasy about the computer's calculations, wants Katherine Johnson to personally check the numbers. Yes, the little girl from West Virginia who loved to count was now a mathematician working for NASA. "Get the girl to check the numbers," Glenn said. "If she says the numbers are good...I'm ready to go."

As America stood on the brink of World War II, the push for space flight advancement grew, which created a constant demand for mathematicians.

1. https://www.nasa.gov/audience/foreducators/a-lifetime-of-stem.html
2. https://www.foxmovies.com/movies/hidden-figures

Women were the solution. Sharp and successful, the female population skyrocketed at the Langley Headquarters of the National Advisory Committee for Aeronautics, NASA's predecessor. "These women were both ordinary and they were extraordinary," says Margot Lee Shetterly, author of the book, *Hidden Figures*.[3]

Katherine Johnson, now with the space task force, became its first published female author, co-authoring the paper that determined the trajectories of the first Mercury flights.[4] This gifted woman was simultaneously shifting the trajectories of destinies of thousands who would come after her as she blazed a trail for generations to come. But she is quoted as saying, "I wasn't aware of all of that, I was just doing my job."

From 1958 until her retirement in 1986, Katherine Johnson worked as an aerospace technologist. She calculated the trajectories for the first American in space, Alan Shepherd's 1961 Mercury mission, and Apollo 11, which put the first men on the moon. She plotted backup navigation charts for astronauts in case of electronic failures. She worked on the Apollo 13 moon mission and when it was aborted, her work on backup procedures and charts helped to set a safe path for the crew's return to earth, creating a one-star observation system that would allow astronauts to determine their location with accuracy. In a 2010 interview, Johnson recalled, "Everybody was concerned about them getting there. We were concerned about them getting back." Later in her career, she worked on the space shuttle program, the Earth Resources Satellite, and on plans for a mission to Mars. In 2015, she received the Presidential Medal of Freedom and in May 2016, a NASA computational research facility was named in her honor in her hometown of Hampton, Virginia.

Of her contributions to NASA, the agency said, "She was a trailblazer, forging a path that would allow many others to follow in her steps. Her spirit and determination helped lead NASA into a new era, and for that the agency is grateful."

---

3. Margot Lee Shetterly, *Hidden Figures: The American Dream and the Untold Story of the Black Women Mathematicians Who Helped Win the Space Race* (New York: William Morrow, 2016)

4. https://ntrs.nasa.gov/search.jsp?R=19980227091

What Lies Ahead?

Is there anyone who desires to always stay where they are today? I think it's safe to say we all want to see what awaits us. Somewhere inside us, we carry a belief that we have a divine destiny, a calling planned for our life that encompasses the purpose we were created to fulfill and places a demand on those parts of us that are essential to who we are as individuals. Every now and then, we catch a glimpse of things that lie just past what our eyes can see today. Stretched out there, still in front of us, lies our dream— the thing we see ourselves doing. There is a voice deep inside of us saying, "There is more to you and for you than your current situation." There is a godly yearning for what we were intended for. Its details are hidden in the unknown, but we are ever pressing toward it.

> *Through followers of Jesus like yourselves gathered in churches, this extraordinary plan of God is becoming known.*
>
> (Ephesians 3:10 MSG)

There is a sense of deep calling to deep, an inner voice beckoning to us, calling us to keep moving forward on this journey of life.

Let me clarify something that might be transpiring in your life right now. The voice inside of you is real. It compels you onward to consider things for your life that your mind can't comprehend as possible. In a "prove it to me" society, it can be easy to forget the reality that not all voices calling to us, leading us from place to place, are audible ones.

We can hear our destiny. We can hear the voice of the Author and Finisher of our faith, the Architect of our purpose, giving directives through the Holy Spirit, our unseen guide. We catch a glimpse with our spiritual eyes of places and possibilities that have yet to be. All of these things speak and they call out to us to continue on a path, a calling designed even before you or I took our first breath.

This path of destiny is not a stagnant path. It is a living path that is a collaborative undertaking between the Creator of the universe and the sons and daughters of God. You are living in a divine partnership with God. His is a gift of a divine life coming from the inside and igniting a blazing light on our shining path, where history is going to be made and your old history is rewritten. It is how legacies are forged to blaze a trail to be found by approaching generations, blowing open brand new doors from the path you have carved.

Jesus Blazed the Trail for Us

Jesus blazed a trail for all of us to follow. He leads the way and gives us our purpose, which is a continuation of what He came to do. What an honor and a task: to expel my life's energy on finishing my Master's course with joy. To stand with Him and hear the Father say to us, "Well done."

Essentially, all mechanisms of travel begin with an impulse that places them on a path in which they go from one point to another. Sometimes, additional impulses assist along the path, if necessary, to keep them on course.

Did you know your destiny has its own DNA? It gravitates toward what you were designed to be. It pulls you toward things with your specific DNA of destiny attached to it to keep you on course. And along this trajectory of destiny, God has reserves in store for you. There is a vast supply along your course because what you are called to do is going to take a great supply. It is beyond what you could ever generate on your own, so He has prepared it and placed it there for you.

> *…What God determined as the way to bring out His best in us, long before we ever arrived on the scene. The experts of our day haven't a clue about what this eternal plan is. If they had, they wouldn't have killed the Master of the God-designed life on a cross. That's why we have this Scripture text: No one's ever seen or heard anything like this, Never so much as imagined anything quite like it—What God has arranged for those who love him. But you've seen and heard it because God by his Spirit has brought it all out into the open before you.*
>
> (1 Corinthians 9–10 MSG)

The Trajectory of Your Destiny

Your destiny follows a specific path—a trajectory much like that plotted by Katherine Johnson, only yours is plotted by God. One definition of trajectory is, "The path followed by a moving object under the action of a given force." You are the moving object and God is the force. Another definition is, "A family of curves or surfaces at a constant angle." For instance, the earth, being round, provides a series of curves or surfaces at a constant angle. When a spacecraft circles the earth, it travels across this series of curves and surfaces. The trajectory of our destiny spans across the earth in a series of curves and turns, ever moving forward. Destiny does not play out in a straight line. The way God is leading you and the path He is directing you to take is not designed to get you quickly from point A to point B. Your destined path will have all kinds of twists and turns because God uses your path to prepare you for your calling—what He is moving you toward.

Take a look with fresh eyes at this verse in the Word of God that Paul was inspired to write:

> *I press toward the mark for the prize of the high calling of God in Christ Jesus.* (Philippians 3:14 KJV)

Notice Paul said he presses toward *"the mark."* Not the prize but the mark. This is a really big key Paul was giving us about how to live. He was saying, "I press toward where God is leading me right now. I'm not just making a mad dash for the finish line." This is so important for us to know and will alleviate so much frustration in our lives. God is going to lead you on a destined path to eventually take you to your dream, but the actual path taking you there is key. In God's way of doing things, the path is equal in value to the prize. He uses the marks to get you ready for the prize. The marks are where learning takes place. God actually prepares us along the way as He takes us to what He has prepared *for* us. How amazingly strategic is our God!? There is purpose in every step of your life toward the prize—and that purpose is servant leadership.

IN GOD'S WAY OF DOING THINGS, THE PATH IS EQUAL IN VALUE TO THE PRIZE.

Other words that describe a "trajectory" are a course, path, route, track, or orbit. It also means "to throw across." This gives us new insight into situations in which we feel like life is throwing us a curve ball. When we realize destiny does not always follow a straight line, it won't throw us off balance when we experience a sudden turn. For people in relationship with God and following His leading, those curve ball moments can be used by God to prepare you. The good news is, we don't have to sweat the curve balls anymore. All along your path is a vast supply that comes with each new step of destiny and faith we take.

Being a hearer, speaker, and doer of the Word will make the difference between going through life the easy way or the hard way. If you speak the word of God as you are walking out in destiny, your supply and every divine connection will be right on time.

It Didn't Start with You

In essence, your life is following a path that's already been in motion. It's part of the trajectories of the generations who came before you. It merely picked you up, kept moving, and now stretches out in front of you.

> YOUR LIFE IS FOLLOWING A PATH THAT'S ALREADY BEEN IN MOTION.

Magnetic currents run under our feet and flow from the North Pole to the South Pole. In the skies above, there are electric currents and vibrations that we are learning to describe and harness. In the spiritual realm and in the words God has spoken, there are currents and trajectories for His plans and purposes that we cannot describe or measure in natural terms.

Three Factors Influence Your Calling

So it is important to understand that your calling, your destiny, is mainly influenced, generally speaking, by three major factors:

1. What has been handed to you.

2. Your new creation experience with God.

3. What you do with it and the decisions you make.

Let's take a look at the first factor, "What been handed to you."

Anna Robertson Brown Lindsay (1864–1948), the first woman to earn a doctorate at the University of Pennsylvania, described it this way:

"Under a thousand shifting generations, there was rising the combination that I today am. In me culminates, for my life's day, human history until now."[5]

This is the first ordeal set before each one of us: to rise above the heredity of the broken places in our family line from those who have gone before us and embrace all of the good, the virtue, and the nobility we have inherited.

Our current culture likes to make much of individuals refusing to be labeled by any definition. However, no one enters into the world as a blank canvas. We all are born with a definition given to us by our Creator.

WE ALL ARE BORN WITH A DEFINITION GIVEN TO US BY OUR CREATOR.

In talking about their destiny, people often ask a question about their lineage, such as, "Am I foreordained to sin?" or "Are there strains of addictions, broken places, and character flaws in me that I'll never go beyond or be able to break out of?"

This leads us to the second factor, your new creation experience with God. We have to understand that when God is given residence within us, He is the Victor who brings triumph over all sin. Sin is at the root of brokenness that may have come because of your sin or the sin of someone else. Regardless, when you give your life to Christ, He comes to take residence in you so you receive your redeemed inheritance. His glory comes into you. Make sure you are convinced of this and read what the Bible says about it.

Even the mystery which hath been hid from ages and from generations, but now is made manifest to his saints: To whom God would make known what is the riches of the glory of this mystery among the Gentiles; which is Christ in you, the hope of glory.

(Colossians 1:26–27 KJV)

When you are saved, you receive Christ in you, the hope of glory. As you yield to Him within you, He changes you. The more you are immersed

---

5. Anna Robertson Brown Lindsay, Ph.D., *The Warrior Spirit in the Republic of God* (New York: The Macmillan Company, 1906)

in the Word of God and yield to the Spirit of God, the more you are changed by what is already inside of you. This is how you can experience, *"Christ in you, the hope of glory."* All that is left is for you, through Him, to be the Victor in all of the great combats in life.

Whatever hardships, battles or opposition we may encounter, it does not have to have the upper hand over our souls when we are in Him because He is triumphant in us. Triumph is not an event but a place of being. Unless we are triumphant, we cannot be truly useful to someone else. It is not the degradation of what has gone on before us that has the trump card over our destiny. It is our heart, will, and faith locked hand in hand with Jesus, working together for victory. The work of my will, heart, and faith is to hold my place in Him in a world whose nature and culture oppose the very Spirit of the One who lives in me.

God has been carrying on His triumph through thousands of generations that have come before you and me. We are a part of this amazing redeemed race of new creatures that we have been born into and this ongoing march of ours. We find ourselves on the front lines with the living generations on the earth. As a person of divine destiny, and a part of the family of God, I feel a wind at my back of all they have believed, declared, and stood for. I now stand in that place because of the force of their love in spite of hate, the ground they took, and the claim they staked. And just like there are flashes and surges of electrical currents of energy, there also runs a current throughout all of mankind's history. It is a current of spiritual power, inspiration, and a move of His Spirit that is now looking to find its voice and its movement through you and me.

Anna Robertson Brown Lindsay wrote:

"The ground we tread was once trodden by the feet of those long dead. I am taking up their room, and in due time, I myself must depart, that there may be footwear for those who are to come after me. Only the ground under me (in this moment) is really mine…"

This is my responsibility. It is the time I have been born into. There is a spirit of courage to believe that rises up inside us and compels us to go the distance and run with focused faith and vitality to reach each and every mark and destined place, to allow for whatever preparation is needed so we will be ready for all God would have us do. Feeling this force of all that has come before us lights a fire in our hearts to see the calling He has given us fulfilled. It allows the Holy Spirit to truly be the source of our dreams that define God's plan for our lives. This force also compels a compassion and love in us for one another, remembering the big picture, that our lives do not stand separated and apart but connecting both our beginning and our ending in this life. It reminds us to travel in kindness, to give generously rather than hang on to what is only temporary.

When I stop and ponder all of this, it makes me realize nothing is too hard, too distasteful, or too insignificant. It stirs in me a sense of duty to do my best. This is His grand path of destiny working through you and me.

Questions to Reflect on:

What lifelong activities have you enjoyed the way Katherine Johnson loved math?

_____

_____

_____

_____

_____

_____

_____

_____

_____

Why does God not give us a straight path to follow to reach our destiny?

_____

_____

_____

_____

_____

_____

_____

_____

_____

What factors influence your calling?

How should we view any hardships we encounter?

CHAPTER 2

BREAKING THE BOX

What do you do when your life doesn't fit the boxes of a felt calling, when what you do does not line up with a direct, more obvious line of "making a difference," when there is no pulpit, no gathering, no momentous event giving expression to what God has placed within you? The nagging question begins to eat at you, in an alarming way: "Where did I go wrong?"

But what if you didn't go wrong at all? What if your "box-lacking" life is exactly where God has been working to bring you?

More times than I can count, I have sat across from individuals who were wrestling with these deep questions.

Our own self-doubt can hide divine destiny from our view. Preconceived ideas can rob you of the colors and vastness of the big picture God is painting in your life. Here we are, in the epicenter of a masterpiece, the subjects of a kingdom masterpiece but unaware of it! And our blindness is coming from the fact that we have limited the vastness of how God wants to use us. We have confined His divine purpose down to the few avenues we envision such a life should look like. We have been too concerned with conventional molds and ways of doing things.

> MEN AND WOMEN OF DESTINY ARE PUT ON THE EARTH IN THEIR TIME
> NOT SO THEIR TIME WOULD MOLD THEM BUT
> SO THEY WOULD MOLD THEIR TIME!

Men and women of destiny are put on the earth in their time not so their time would mold them but so they would mold their time! The world we live in must change and progress because we have not yet reached our best. To make things better and find better ways of doing things, someone has to lead the way. Someone has to go first!

To Lead by Influencing Rather Than Imposing

For too long, men and women of God have relinquished positions of influence, where real answers can be given and change can take place, because we thought it was deemed unspiritual business. Nothing could be further from the truth. The word of God commanded us to go forth and have dominion, not by imposing but rather by influence. To be in the rooms where important conversations are being held because we have answers. We should be seeking places of leading in every part of our culture and not shrinking back from that. True ambition is the soul's reaching out toward preordained things! It's the nature of God inside of us that says we should be great and do great. We should be ever redefining the way things are done because of the Greater One who lives within us. Revelation is always progressing and so should we as people of destiny!

Even in nature, when an acorn falls, no one expects it to grow into something small and low to the ground. No, we expect it to become a strong, mighty oak tree! In the same way, God doesn't say to us, "I don't expect you to become much or do much. Just exist as meekly as you can." Just the opposite! We are supposed to reach for high things and look for mold-breaking ways God wants us to move forward.

Residing within our spirit are the rumblings and echoes of our big brother Jesus's victorious domination and triumph over death, hell, and the grave. These rumblings and stirrings of our King, Jesus within us, are in the DNA of our destiny, just awaiting the chance to come alive and affect the generation you and I are living in, to take dominion over works of the kingdom over darkness, to reveal, by influence and example, the kingdom of God to people.

The truth is, if you are only looking at the boxes existing right now, you will never break out from them. For instance, one person might spend their time looking down at their shoes while another is constantly looking up and all around for opportunity.

Living from the Big Picture

The first step toward embracing your place of influence is thinking big. This is so powerful in our lives because when we pull back and see the big picture, it gives the Holy Spirit a broad canvas to paint on to show you how God wants to use you and position you. We have to receive our assignment for life by faith; we can't filter it through our natural understanding because it is going to come through revelation from the Holy Spirit.

What is revelation? Simply put, it is seeing. *"For all the land that you see I will give to you and to your offspring forever"* (Genesis 13:15 esv).

God has designed you and me to see new ways of doing things. When men and women of destiny are innovators, the result is that we can bless humanity.

Innovation is our secret weapon. We were made to be innovators because we are divinely connected to heaven's limitless revelation. We have access to answers. In this way, leadership belongs to those who believe.

The call of Jesus to everyone involves our work—what we do with our lives here on earth. His is not a call to rest *from* work but to rest *in* work. In fact, we can accomplish more and do even more because He lives in us. As men and women of God, there is a higher element to what we do vocationally. There is a divinely inspired creativity and innovation dynamic that makes an art of whatever we do.

Others May Not Share Our Dreams

There is a great scene in one of my all-time favorite movies from when I was a kid; it is a classic in our family, growing up with all brothers who were avid baseball players. In the 1989 movie *Field of Dreams*, Iowa farmer Ray (Kevin Costner) hears a mysterious voice one day while working in his field: "If you build it, he will come." Eventually, he comes to the revelation that what this voice is compelling him to do is mow down part of his crops and build a baseball field. Finally, he does it. It threatens to cost him everything he has, but at the end of the movie, the purpose becomes clear as it all leads to Ray and his father re-connecting and restoring their twenty-year broken relationship over a game of catch.

> ## WHAT GOD IS DOING WITH YOUR LIFE IS NOT JUST FOR YOU BUT FOR GENERATIONS TO COME.

This is how God moves. He pours the foundation so He can build without limits, regardless of the fact that others cannot yet see it. He positions us so He can propel. He digs deep so He can build high. And what He builds in and through our lives lasts long after we are gone. What He is doing with your life is not just for you but for generations to come. Sometimes just saying what you see is the beginning point. It serves as the burden of proof that God is revealing to you a new way of doing things that is meant to make a difference.

Too many times, the seemingly mundane robs us of our sense of destiny. As believers and as the church of Jesus Christ, we have to return to our original calling, which He authored, to be agents of change in the world we live in. When heaven looks at what is happening on the earth, it is not solely zeroed in on Sunday morning gatherings. The kingdom of God is not ONLY being expanded within the four walls of the church. Don't get me wrong—we are the church. And the church of Jesus Christ is God's idea, not man's. The church is His bride and it is still "the most powerful force of any nation," as Dr. Mary Frances Varallo[6] puts it. But the church is where we come to become all that Jesus made us to be.

If your calling requires a pulpit or a church platform or takes place in a church building, then you most predominantly are an equipper. You are called to help to equip the body of Christ. This is a powerful, significant calling and an honor. It takes quite a lot of work for a local church to be effective at discipling and equipping.

---

6. http://maryfrancesvaralloministries.com

If your calling does not require a pulpit or church platform or take place within a church building, you, my friend, are most predominantly called as an agent of change. In some way or another, we are all called to take part in both, but one will outweigh the other in your life, depending on how God has positioned you. It is our highest honor in life that we are called to either, but the former exists for the benefit of the latter. This is quite the upside paradigm from merely wandering through the work week until Sunday. In reality, the most pivotal thing you do to be an influence for the kingdom of God is happening Monday through Friday.

> **THE MOST PIVOTAL THING YOU DO TO IMPACT THE KINGDOM IS HAPPENING MONDAY THROUGH FRIDAY.**

The bottom line is this: what God is doing on earth is meant to happen everywhere! This is where God places His called ones—everywhere! There is a tremendous life change that happens in our churches, but we must awaken to the whole realm of activity taking place in every facet of the world we live in. All of it is significant! All of it matters. God has called the preacher and the school principal. A sense of mission belongs to all of us, not just those called to the five-fold ministry. As part of the kingdom of God, our purpose and our sense of calling in life would be so much greater if we would awaken each day with a sense of being that says, "God, You know what lies before me today and all the responsibilities I face. Even still, I am Yours to command. Lead me."

The Story of Oscar's Trunks

A couple of weeks before Thanksgiving, I was home for just three days in between speaking engagements and was busy preparing to host my out-of-town family for the holiday. I was enjoying a quiet morning, drinking a cup of coffee, so happy to be home for a few days. I was looking on my phone at a local page that had items for sale. I had my eye out for a fire pit for my backyard.

As I scrolled through the items for sale, I came across these two beautiful, medium-sized, leather box trunks with a black and white inlay down the center. I stopped for a moment to look at them—they were so beautiful and unique—but then continued on with my search for a fire pit. To tell you the truth, what I felt next in my heart in the next moment was so slight, it was just like a quick flash across my heart: "Go back and buy those boxes." The thought immediately seemed strange. "Buy those boxes? What do I want with those boxes?"

I did really like them. They were beautiful but, I thought, sort of unnecessary. I scrolled back and looked at them again, still scratching my head at the idea; it all seemed just so out of left field. But then sure enough, it came up in me again: "Buy those boxes." This was all just so very odd! I had so much to do that day and very little time to get it all done. I was all set to be a woman on a mission that day to get my pre-holiday to-do list accomplished, but there was this pervading nudge in my gut. Finally, I thought to myself, "Well, worst case scenario, I am just totally missing it and the only one who will know will be me." I clicked the link and made arrangements to purchase the boxes.

As it turned out, after I purchased the boxes, I found out the pick-up point was about a forty-five minute drive from my house! My frustration intensified. This was going to eat up so much of my time, which I didn't have to spare. But now, I was stuck.

This was all so strange! Why did I feel so drawn toward these specific trunks and for what purpose? As I drove through the city and headed north to the outskirts of town, I thought again, "Why did I do this? I am totally wasting time when I have so much to get done." All the way there, I reprimanded myself for not thinking things through a little better. This was not living my "best life!"

"Hello There, Woman of God."

When I arrived at the location, a lovely woman greeted me with a big smile. She immediately stood out to me because of her perfect complexion and beautiful olive skin. I, on the other hand, had opted for the "hair in a ponytail, jeans, and sweater" look for the day. At her first words, I immediately regretted it. She came toward me, smiling, and said, "Hello there, woman of God."

Did I know her? Should I know her? What am I even doing here?

She took my hand and said, "My daughter and I saw your name and she told me about your book, *Your Defining Moment*. So we looked you up on the Internet. Wow! My daughter told me, 'Mom, this is your day. God set this up for you today.'"

Right then, the realization hit me: this was no ordinary Tuesday morning and these were no ordinary trunks. I responded, somewhat awkwardly, and asked her where she was from. She began to tell me her story. She and her family were from a country in the Middle East. While they lived there, through a series of circumstances, she found out her daughter had secretly become a Christian and had been attending an underground church gathering that was meeting privately. She said, "It wasn't long after that when I, too, became a Christian and started going to the meetings as well." But eventually, word had been leaked that she and her daughter had become Christians and now their lives were in danger. Soon afterward, a way was made and they both fled for the United States. I stood there, amazed at what I was hearing and the courage of this mother and her daughter.

She continued, "But I know that God sent you here today because of the battle we are in for the life of my little grandson, Oscar." Her eyes filled with tears and my heart immediately went out to her. When she said the name "Oscar," I knew whatever the situation was, this is exactly why I was there.

I took her hands and asked her to tell me about little Oscar. Through tears, she began to explain, "He is only two years old and has been in critical care with a life-threatening condition." Reaching for her phone, she began showing me photos of her beloved grandson. I saw the love in her eyes as she said, "Look at my little Oscar. You can tell he is special, can you not?" Knowing how all grandmothers feel about their grandbabies, I smiled back and looked at little Oscar's picture. In all honesty, she was absolutely right. He was truly one of the most beautiful, happy little boys I had ever seen. He had a full head of soft, black, curly hair. He had his grandmother's perfect olive skin, with big dark eyes and long eyelashes. His big smile was contagious, even in a photo, and lit up his whole face. He looked like a little angel. To look at this picture, you would never know anything was wrong with this precious child. I looked back at Oscar's grandmother and said, "He truly is quite special. The hand of God is on his life."

She smiled. "And oh, how my boy loves to pray! He insists we pray every night! He hears me pray and I just know that God is making the way for my grandson. I have been asking Him to send me someone that would stand in agreement with me for Him and then I knew it would be done. And so, today, when my daughter looked you up and said, 'Mom this is your day, something is happening for us,' I knew in my heart, God had sent the one I had been asking for, that you would pray and agree with me for my grandson Oscar to be well."

We joined our hands together and Oscar's grandmother and I bowed our heads and began to pray. We declared healing for Oscar because of what Jesus had done for him and spoke the life of God into Oscar's body. We declared his heart and lungs to be whole and commanded all forms of disease to leave his body in Jesus's name. Then I prayed the blessing of the Lord over her and her precious family, that they would have so much to be thankful for over the upcoming Thanksgiving weekend. When we said, "Amen," we both looked at each other and hugged with tears rolling down our faces.

I said, "How amazing is God to use these trunks to bring us together today!" She said, "He heard my prayer and I feel so filled with joy about it all!"

I loaded the trunks into my car and hugged her goodbye. As we parted, she said, "And please, may you think of my Oscar every time you look at these boxes and declare over him." I promised her that there was no way I would forget that day and I most definitely would.

I got back into my car and began driving the forty-five minutes back home in total amazement. What an experience! All of that was connected to the still, small voice of the Lord, getting my attention and in essence, just saying, "Would you do something for Me today? Would you trust Me with your agenda and stop to take care of something that is important to Me?"

The ironic thing was, all the way there, I had complained to myself about what a waste of time this was. But all the way home, I cried tears of gratefulness, thanking Him for allowing me to be a part of something He was orchestrating in someone else's life.

There are things on our Father's heart today and He is searching for someone who will say, "Here am I...send me." Sure, God sends people around the world, but it could be God is asking you to go just few miles up the road.

GOD IS WEAVING DESTINY EVERY DAY IN A MILLION DIFFERENT WAYS.

God is weaving destiny every day in a million different ways. He is using any means necessary to get people exactly what they need. On that particular day, no pulpit, public gathering, or grand commissioning was required. Just the still, small voice of the Holy Spirit saying, "I want you to buy those trunks."

This is the activity of heaven—to reveal to you how you are meant or called to impact your generation. For years, the enemy has attempted to demoralize a large majority of believers, making them believe the lie that they were unemployed in the great business of heaven.

There is a life-long journey that we are all on as believers and that is a journey of knowing God and all the many facets of Him, to grow in that relationship and know Him more intimately every day. But that is only half of the equation of your life as a believer.

The other half is what you are called to do with what you have become. It is so important that you understand that God will place you, position you, and use you. And all of the ways He has for doing this are as vast as the ocean. He is limitless in the ways He will use your skill, abilities, know-how, and personality to influence, invigorate, and shift things each and every day. You are made in the image and likeness of God. When God saw darkness, He brought the Light into it and changed it. We are just like Him. We are made to change things and bring the Light into the darkness. If God didn't settle for "this is just how it's always been," then neither should we!

Living with this big picture in mind will produce something really beautiful. The sum of your life will amount to a great tapestry of destiny moments that changed things beyond what you could see at the time. This is God's business. Destiny is His business, His specialty, and He is constantly working all around you and me. We just get the thrill of being a part of it if we will yield to it.

God is much bigger than whatever box you may have been stuck in related to His call upon you. So many people get caught up in their past. Your calling has not been erased because of the life choices you've made or haven't made. If you have made a commitment to Him and His plan for you, then you are right now in the palm of His hand. He is taking you from faith to faith and glory to glory. He has sustained you and if you awaken to it, He will set you up for influence in a greater way than you ever thought probable for your life! I have watched Him do this time and time again.

Let us be the generation that breaks the boxes limiting our callings; let's fully embrace our divine invitation for service. We have each been invited into the service of the kingdom of God, to participate with heaven, right here on the earth, to bring light into the darkness. Your life is an opportunity to participate in this grand collaboration in whatever way He gives you.

YOUR LIFE IS AN OPPORTUNITY TO PARTICIPATE IN THIS GRAND COLLABORATION.

I would encourage you to do two things. First, take the time to ask God about how He wants to use the abilities He has given you. Remember that whatever you have a passion for is usually an avenue God desires to work through and whatever you have a compassion for is typically what you are called to do something about. Secondly, decide now to be a person God can work through on a daily basis. Start your days with the internal posture that says, "Here am I, God, send me. I am willing and I am Yours to command today."

Years ago, I took a road trip with a very dear friend of mine to Ponca City, Oklahoma. She had purchased a new car and we were picking it up at a dealership there. The city has a museum and statue dedicated to the Pioneer Woman.[7] The statue's face is lit up and her eyes are sharply focused. She has a Bible under her right arm and her left hand is holding

---

7. http://www.okhistory.org/sites/pioneerwoman

the hand of a young boy. She is the epitome of a woman on a mission. The women pioneers in her day took the Bible as the book for their very lives. They infused it into almost everything they did. They found the courage they needed to find new and innovative ways to live and survive. And they passed its principles down to their children. They walked with courage and faith toward a better day.

This is the spirit of people of destiny that carved the way for a nation. It is the only way for us to continue on into our future.

As believers and, collectively, as the body of Christ, it is now time for our focus to shift to mobilizing all of the callings sitting in the pews. It's time to turn our attention, as individuals, to how we can reach out instead of waiting to be called out. Let's shake ourselves loose from the old patterns and allow revelation to take us into a divine transformation of our culture through those He has called: all of us.

Questions to Reflect on:

What preconceived ideas have you had that may have been keeping you from realizing part of your calling?

_____

_____

_____

_____

_____

_____

_____

_____

_____

In what ways can you see that God is wanting to use you through your typical Monday through Friday week?

_____

_____

_____

_____

_____

_____

_____

_____

_____

What changes can you make to better position yourself to hear and recognize God's voice speaking to you?

_____

_____

_____

_____

_____

_____

_____

_____

_____

_____

_____

_____

_____

_____

_____

_____

_____

_____

_____

_____

_____

_____

_____

CHAPTER 3

THE CHANGING OF THE GUARD

Who's to say that things need to change?"

This is the first telltale thought that jumps to the mind of anyone with their head stuck in the sand when change is brought up. But change is already here! Whether we think change is needed or not is irrelevant. Things *are* changing. Things have been changing. And things will continue to change, only more rapidly. The real hope for any changes that *we* make—whether in our personal lives, our businesses, churches, or ministries—is that the change will cause things to grow, that new innovations will give birth to brand new places of success.

What is innovation? Maybe we all think we have a pretty good grip on what it means, but let's take a closer look:

1. Innovation, as defined by Wikipedia, is the application of better solutions that meet new requirements, unarticulated needs, or existing needs.

2. Innovation takes place through the provision of more effective products, processes, services, technologies, or models of operation.

3. Innovation is related to, but not the same as, invention.

So innovation, simply put, is all about better solutions and better ways of doing things to meet new needs. More importantly, innovation causes things to grow.

The biggest roadblock to innovation is aversion to change. Change can feel like an archnemesis to those who have experienced success in the past. Maybe we made just the right move at just the right moment and the result was success. "Well done," we're told, and the "win," so to speak, is pinned on us like a medal.

But now the moment has passed. The reality sets in that brand new cycles of "moments" have arrived, with new needs requiring new moves because there are new battles at hand. And what brought home the win the last time isn't necessarily what it's going to take this time.

THE WORLD IS LOOKING FOR PEOPLE WITH ANSWERS TO MEET THE NEEDS OF TODAY AND TOMORROW, NOT YESTERDAY.

The truth is, the world is looking for people with answers to meet the needs of today and tomorrow, not yesterday. In essence, the world is looking around and asking, "Who has the answer for this moment?" and "Who possesses what I need to make it today?" Like a ship looking for a captain, the world and our culture need a steady hand at the wheel of influence.

But who are these potential influencers of spirituality, commerce, society, and thought? What pools of potential are they coming from? Those who call themselves believers in Christ and proponents of His kingdom must ask themselves, "Am I a part of leading the change in my avenues of life? Or am I waiting to be told what the changes will be by forces that feel more formidable than me?"

We should be asking ourselves these questions on a large scale. Who is leading our nation and the world? Who is writing the songs? Who is creating the stories appearing on our screens? Who is sitting on the school board? Who is running the community group? Among people I know, who does everyone look to for answers—and why? From the pastor to the principal, from the mother to the mayor, and from the grocer to the governor, everyone has a voice for influence.

The world is changing. Out of this river of change, something is singing out a song for each of us to hear. It's calling us, asking us to move the riverbanks, make the river wider or deeper, and remove dams and debris.

For a moment, let's take an honest look at why we sometimes cling to the feeling of relief compelling us to keep repeating what we have always done. Sticking to the old way of doing things holds us safely in a place we already know. It builds a castle of self-preservation for us. The guesswork, the disruption, the element of surprise, and all of those awkward feelings of starting over are removed from our psyche, bringing sweet relief to our humanity.

But there is a danger that comes from living in self-preservation mode: you can preserve yourself into a relic frozen in time! If we live in a state of fear of what change will bring, then we better take a good look around us and make sure we like it, because that's as far as we are ever going to go and all we are ever going to be. It may be fine for a while, but if we let our humanity take the lead, we can too easily ride on the wins of days gone by and be falsely emboldened for the battles of today. If we are not willing to innovate, we are setting ourselves up to fail. This state of being without fresh eyes and ears is not the condition the Word of God calls us to live in.

Our humanity wants to dig in its heels and grip the reins of our experiences. But just because our humanity rises up doesn't mean we have to yield to its tantrums. We have to rise above the test of our flesh.

Addicted to a False Sense of Peace

If we are not careful, we can become addicted to the false peace that comes from whatever brings comfort to our flesh. A safe, easy job. A feel-good church. A hollow relationship. False peace is so dangerous to your life's calling because it will almost subconsciously influence you to steer clear of anything that would ignite the unknown or might potentially place a demand on your deepest reservoirs of faith, strength, and endurance.

We were made for going after things and taking hold of things courageously by faith. We were made to be known as audaciously bold people of strength because of Christ in us. We were made to win battles, not peace-filled expeditions. We are called as a deeply passionate people who live and do everything out of our hearts.

As believers, we were made to care the most, to feel things deeply, to be so moved with compassion that we act boldly. We were made to instigate change. We are the family of God, yes, but we are also the army of God and that takes *more*.

The Bible version of peace and people who are peace-makers can be volatile. Angry people often have trouble understanding them. Jesus Himself is the Prince of Peace and yet everywhere He went, He disrupted the false peace, throwing things into temporary chaos. Why? To initiate a new way of doing things that would inaugurate true peace. Jesus taught us how to make peace.

Blessed are the peacemakers, for they shall be called the sons of God.
(Matthew 5:9 ESV)

In our current western culture, how many days can we live without being disturbed about anything? If you have a reasonable amount of money, don't watch or read much news, avoid getting too deeply involved in anything, and merely go about your life staying in the shallow places, other than an occasional traffic jam, you could live almost all of your days in an undisturbed sense of peace—peaceful to your humanity, that is. But as believers in Christ, I don't think we really want to live undisturbed. When we get down to what matters in life, we want to be disturbed by what is on the heart of our Father. We want to be disrupted by a vision He has placed in us that compels us. We want to be disturbed by what is happening in the generation we are called to lead. If I am *undisturbed*, I will feel no need for change and I will slip slowly into ineffectiveness. That is not a state I can live with.

So before we get stuck in a place because we are jousting with everything that disrupts our lives as "not having peace about it," let's stop and remember that making peace can sometimes mean temporarily having what feels like chaos. Something must disrupt and confront the current state of things so you and the Holy Spirit can get things in a new order and become productive, fruitful, and successful, today.

At first, the words coming to your heart from the Spirit of God can sound unsettling. They will call your attention to whatever has stopped you from progressing. These words or "internal knowings" are giving you something higher than mere information; they are giving you the revelation, "This old way must go."

If you are like me, then your next thought is, "And replace it with what?" The temptation can be to do nothing because we don't have an immediate answer. But that is not how pruning happens. First you cut, then you remove. Then and only then, the new can spring forth.

Jesus said:

Every branch in Me that does not bear fruit [the Father] takes away; and every branch that bears fruit He prunes, that it may bear more fruit. (John 15:2)

World-renowned economist Joseph Schumpeter is called the father of "creative destruction." This is the theory that innovation sustains growth by destroying old ways of doing things. There is a lot reverberating in this line of thought from the prophet Jeremiah:

And it shall come to pass, that as I have watched over them to pluck up, to break down, to throw down, to destroy, and to afflict, so I will watch over them to build and to plant, says the LORD. (Jeremiah 31:28)

Destruction comes before construction and tearing down comes before growth. The reality is, we are called to affect our world, but to accomplish this, we have to be willing to endure a new disruption. We can see the confines we've been living in and the ceiling over our heads. We need to find the courage to rise up and say, "We can't stay here—because there is more."

For those of us who were raised in a legacy of family, business, or even ministry, this isn't as clear-cut as it sounds. What we are talking about here is a rebirth of methods, not principles—unless your principles came from religious, man-invented ideas and not the Word of God. There is a big difference. Choosing innovation can mean letting go of ways of doing things handed down to us from our predecessors and choosing instead to look to the Spirit of Truth on the inside for how He would lead us to go. Not all plans are meant to continue forever. Some are seasonal; some are generational. If we are going to be a vibrant part of the building of the Kingdom of God, we have to listen and obey His voice, not just duplicate the blueprint from yesterday.

The danger of merely duplicating an earlier version of living and leading is it can entangle us in a false sense of loyalty while cutting off our vital union with the Holy Spirit for receiving His directives. His job is to lead the body of Christ—you and me.

Leery of the Promise of False Peace

Jeremiah was living in a time that called for answers. The spiritual leaders called a general assembly to hear from the Lord and determine what had to be done. The oppressive king of Babylon still had some of the people of Judah enslaved. The leading prophets of the day were Jeremiah and Hananiah. The latter spoke first:

> *Thus speaks the Lord of hosts, the God of Israel, saying: "I have broken the yoke of the king of Babylon. Within two full years I will bring back to this place all the vessels of the Lord's house...all the captives of Judah who went to Babylon."* (Jeremiah 28:2–4)

Wow. Pretty big statement.

As the prophet Jeremiah stood to respond to this promise of peace, you can almost hear the hesitation in his words. He replied:

> *Amen! The Lord do so; the Lord perform your words which you have prophesied.... Nevertheless hear now this word that I speak in your hearing and in the hearing of all the people: The prophets who have been before me and before you of old prophesied against many countries and great kingdoms—of war and disaster and pestilence. As for the prophet who prophesies of peace, when the word of the prophet comes to pass, the prophet will be known as one whom the Lord has truly sent.* (Jeremiah 28:6–9)

In his reply, you get the sense that Jeremiah was almost giving Hananiah a second chance. Did he really mean that his words were from the Lord?

But Hananiah responded confidently, declaring, *"Thus says the Lord..."* (Jeremiah 28:11).

Jeremiah then left, but the Lord told him to go back and tell Hananiah the truth. He had made the people *"trust in a lie. Therefore thus says the Lord: 'Behold, I will cast you from the face of the earth. This year you shall die, because you have taught rebellion against the* Lord.'" (Jeremiah 28:15–16). And Hananiah, the false prophet, died that same year.

People are so glad to hear words of reprieve. *Words* of peace give us hope for *works* of peace. In this story in the book of Jeremiah, false words of peace put a fierce yoke on the people. Previously, God said, they had yokes of wood, but since they put their faith in a false sense of peace that would require nothing of them, they now had yokes of iron. (See Jeremiah 28:13–14.)

Before they listened to Hananiah, there is no doubt what they were facing—their yokes of wood—would have been broken by following the true Word of God. A yoke of iron, however, is unbreakable. Hananiah's words were detrimental to their thinking. They removed any surge rising up from within them for instigating change. His words set them back into "sit and wait" mode, which brought about a worse bondage than they had before. This was not what God was setting them up for. He had wanted them to rise.

If we shy away from words that instigate change, we are doomed to a yoke ourselves. The problem is, if you carry a yoke long enough, you become so used to it that it becomes the norm, even if it's heavy and burdensome.

Today, we need to have a changing of the guard and people who walk in change. We need new assignments, new ways of doing things, and new individuals added to the ranks to take their place. This isn't for the sake of replacing individuals; it's so every one of us can surge forward. We need to change our thinking, our ways of living, and our ways of leading. We need to let go of how we used to do things. Our trust and confidence of things turning out right cannot stand in old successes more than they stand in Him.

This changing of the guard is about progress—and our provision lies in our progression.

It must stand the test of time, but time cannot dictate the present. It doesn't matter how things have been, or what age anyone is or isn't. We all have a part in this progressive march of the kingdom so long as we pick up His cadence and keep walking with Him.

Leaders in the current generations—Baby Boomers, Generation X, and the Millennials— carry the gifts of invention and innovation. The prior generations of leaders were pioneers and inventors; their natural reaction to purpose was to launch out and start new things. In the Body of Christ, preachers like Billy Graham launched major ministries to reach the world at large. Now, others are pioneering new worlds of ministry.

Millennials and Generation Z are all about innovation, finding better ways of doing things, and looking for ways to implement change. They are wired to question and reach their highest potential. Their needs demand a changing of the guard.

Innovation Seizes the Day

David saw change was needed on the day of his battle against Goliath, so he chose to leave behind the armor and sword passed down to his generation. He did not run to the battlefield to match his opponent weapon for weapon or strategy for strategy. Instead, David went after the giant with vitality, innovation, and change. Goliath was not prepared for that.

The slingshot was not known as a high-grade weapon, but David had grown quite accustomed to this new way of winning. The world at large had never seen such a display of smaller overcoming greater, but they were not prepared for what David had to unleash that day. David didn't invent the slingshot, but he reimagined it. He innovated its use and became very good at it. (See 1 Samuel 17:32–50.)

For those called to lead in our times, there can be no hesitation, reservation, or fear. What if the ways God has been preparing for you look, sound, and operate like nothing you have observed from others? Is the awkward feeling of doing things differently for the first time enough to intimidate you to stumble backwards and plant your feet firmly in the known? Is it enough to cause you to tuck away the dream in your heart and forget it, replacing it with the sights and sounds of the masses? Or will you lead courageously and run to the battle, even when it means everything is on the line?

A Changing of the Guard

In order to *have* change, there must *be* change. Change has to *be* instigated. It is not a force propelled by its own engine. Something or someone must force it into existence, intentionally or not. Sometimes, we do things that unknowingly spark a change we didn't see, or we experience a change we did not instigate. For the most part, however, change takes place because of a decision that originated with you and me. Wise counsel will tell you change takes time. But for the timer to start ticking, someone has to hit start!

As a leader, influencer, and thought-provoker of the kingdom of God, we have to be willing for change to *be* so we can influence effectively. The world is waiting for it.

For all creation, gazing eagerly as if with outstretched neck, is waiting and longing to see the manifestation of the sons of God.

(Romans 8:19 wey)

I love the picture this evokes. Scripture is confirming what we know and see today. There is a leadership vacuum and creation is looking all around, waiting for the called ones to show up and fill it. And fill it we must. We are agents of change and if the generations align, there is no stopping the body of Christ. We are wired and generationally timed for a supernatural overhaul of reaching the world with the person of Jesus Christ. We are called to inaugurate a new way of living in the lives of those we touch.

When we don't, the wrong voices fill these places of influence with hidden agendas. Deceiving pictures are painted to stir up action, but all is not as it seems. People with good-hearted compassion and young vitality are being deceived and led to march for causes that are nothing more than an ends to a means.

But even among a sea of imposters of compassion and thieves of passion, there remains a true and real call for a new shifting and change. There is a true justifiable sense that God is leading us into places where "we have not walked this way before."

We never know what God will use to bring what He is saying or doing to our attention. I once heard a well-known minister suggest that God will sometimes even use Hollywood to convey a message through a movie, story, or song. This is not always the case, but I have felt God speaking to me in this way.

There was a very ethereal song released in 1978 by a young Bob Dylan, during a period when he was a born-again Christian. Within the lyrics is a call coming from a lost, broken, and hurting generation that has grown weary of current conditions. The younger generations today are experiencing these same feelings:

"Gentlemen, he said, I don't need your organization, I've shined your shoes

I've moved your mountains and marked your cards

But Eden is burning, either getting ready for elimination

Or else your hearts must have the courage for the changing of the guards."[8]

When I first read these lyrics, my eyes filled with tears. I hear in them the brokenness of a generation where the enemy has perpetuated a gap and created a group of the disenfranchised. But it is also a call for the restoration of fathers to the son in these words: "your hearts must have courage for the changing of the guards." In them, I hear the cry of a young man saying, "Fight for us. Please do what is needed to come and get us."

Old Definition vs. New Definition

Usually, "the changing of the guard" means an individual or group charged with a task or responsibility is *replaced* by another individual or group. It can also refer to a ceremony in which soldiers or other officials stationed at a major government installation are replaced by a *new shift*.

I was recently in London with just enough time to visit a few places in between my meetings. I saw Winston Churchill's War Rooms, 10 Downing Street in Westminster, and Buckingham Palace. My friend and I arrived at the palace just in time to witness the Changing of the Guard. Watching this ceremony, with the soldiers in their full dress uniforms, you feel a sense of awe. Even though you know they do this often, with shift changes throughout the day, you cannot shake the sense that you are witnessing something noble and important playing out before your eyes. People come from all over the world to wait and watch this ceremony from behind the tall black and gold iron gates of Buckingham Palace. They film

8. Bob Dylan, *"Changing of the Guards,"* on *Street-Legal* (Columbia Records, 1978)

it on their phones to show people back home. For these few minutes, all of the attention and focus is on the Changing of the Guard.

I believe what God is looking for in *our* changing of the guard is not a replacement agenda, but a new guard with an innovative new way of doing things. That means growth—and change.

To have a frame of mind for change, you must recognize that you are not defined by a time period. Made in the image and likeness of God, your spirit, the real you, is eternal. Do not let fear of any change take hold of you because time has no right to define the real you. You are made to influence and affect things every day that you are alive on this earth.

> ## DO NOT LET FEAR OF ANY CHANGE TAKE HOLD OF YOU BECAUSE TIME HAS NO RIGHT TO DEFINE THE REAL YOU.

This vital movement of change instigated by the Holy Spirit is meant to awaken us to our dependency on Him and His leading, not on our past successes or failures.

> *As it is written, "What no eye has seen, nor ear heard, nor the heart of man imagined, what God has prepared for those who love him"—these things God has revealed to us through the Spirit.*
>
> (1 Corinthians 2:9–10 ESV)

"What no eye has seen" cannot take shape while we continue to do what we have done in the past and be who we've always been. We have to forget all of that; our former days cannot give us a roadmap for what lies ahead. We need to use the strength and wisdom we've gained from the past to propel us forward without getting stuck in time.

This is not a new thought. The idea of learning from the past dates back to the oldest stories in the Word of God. Jesus put it simply: *"Remember Lot's wife"* (Luke 17:32).

The Holy Spirit inspired the writers to carry this truth on so we might understand its preeminence. We cannot afford to lead by looking back or leaning on the ways used to get us this far. Our calling is to take part in the changing of the guard. We must be in the change, with the change, willing for the change, become the change, and lead the change. And like David, we will win.

In our ministries, churches, and vocations, there are brand new ways that God wants to show us to express and exemplify His kingdom. The only way to see this is to make room for it and get off the page of what has always been. We must abandon all of our default settings and let God show us something brand new.

The Holy Spirit within you is always ahead of the curve. He knows where *you* have to go, whether it's in your family, your ministry, your business, your career, or all of these.

He knows what lies ahead. The only times I find myself having "trouble with the curve" is when I get unhooked from Him. Then things get rocky and cloudy. But the good news is, the fix is easy and it's on my end. I line back up with the Spirit of truth on the inside of me and together, He and I boldly go where maybe no one has gone before. He gives me courage for the changing of the guard, to be a catalyst for courageous change in my own life, and all that I am called to affect.

Questions to Reflect on:

What has held you back from making changes in your life?

How can you become a voice for influence?

Why is a false sense of peace so detrimental?

_____

_____

_____

_____

_____

_____

_____

_____

_____

_____

What comes to your mind or heart when you consider a changing of the guard?

_____

_____

_____

_____

_____

_____

_____

_____

_____

_____

_____

CHAPTER 4

TRANSITIONS

It happened to be spring break in Panama City Beach, Florida, and I was sitting at a traffic light. It was a major intersection and a very busy rush hour. You get the picture—traffic tie-ups everywhere.

While sitting there, my mind went to some major life decisions I had been contemplating for a few months, one of which involved a major geographical move. There was still so much I didn't know. But I felt that my time of contemplation was quickly coming to an end and the necessity to act was coming fast upon me.

In essence, I was living in a season of transition. These seasons are very interesting. Because the sense of transition is always lingering right under the surface, it winds up affecting every area of our life, albeit unseen. Corporate coaches tell employees who are taking personality and aptitude tests that if they are in a season of transition, they are likely to test out as split into two different categories. Even the "sense" of transitions in life can have an impact on us.

Staring straight ahead at the scene in front of me and the massive number of cars passing by and crisscrossing the intersection, I heard the still small voice of God speak to my heart. He said, "Most accidents in life happen in seasons of transition."

Boom. There it was—a powerful truth. Right in front of me was a play-by-play of all these people trying to get from one place to the next. Some were waiting their turn, others taking their turn, and some taking their turn when it wasn't theirs to take! Risky business! I saw it so clear. Transitions are so pivotal in life and if you are not alert and aware in that season, it can cause you a world of hurt. It is a season that requires your eyes to be wide open.

Interestingly, this season of transition for me began with an unpleasant experience.

Truth Can Be Unsettling

It wasn't so much an event as it was a slow unfolding inside of me. I was in the midst of a busy travel schedule and I slowly came into a place of deep unsettling. I had gone through the usual mental checklist, trying to locate the issue, thinking, "Okay, what is happening here?" But I could not seem to place my finger on the culprit.

Finally, one morning, I woke up to the same dull gnawing on the inside, but this time, I heard these words: "Unsettled by a quiet truth."

"Yes!" my heart shouted. This defined exactly what I was feeling. Unsettled. But by what truth? What was my truth?

A truth can be unsettling because it goes against some form of internal bias you already have. It is unsettling because even while it's undefined, it challenges something on the inside of you. The question is, do you have the courage to seek out what the unsettling truth is and what it is trying to show you?

If I truly believe what the Word of God tells me, that the truth will set me free (John 8:32), then that internal compass compels me to seek out truth. And sometimes, truth is a journey that is more than likely taking you down a path of transition.

SOMETIMES, TRUTH IS A JOURNEY
TAKING YOU DOWN A PATH OF TRANSITION.

The first step in navigating a season of transition is eliminating the bias—that is, anything you think is actually providing your security in place of God.

In chapter thirty-one in the book of Isaiah, this prophet of God lays it out pretty clearly:

> *Woe to them that go down to Egypt for help; and stay on horses, and trust in chariots, [just] because they are many; and in horsemen, [just] because they are very strong; but they look not unto the Holy One of Israel, neither seek the Lord!* (Isaiah 31:3 AMP)

Can you hear the challenge in this verse? Woe to you who live out of a bias about what or who has the power to secure you just because you can add up its numerical value or are impressed by its natural strength. Woe to you who go to the flesh for security and not the more powerful realm of the Spirit.

In seasons of transition, that unsettling truth challenges what you thought you knew. But this is the progression of revelation in our lives helping us walk out each transition. We see now what we did not see before. That truth unravels a bias we once had and frees us to see as God sees and to walk in His liberty. God, in His great love for us, deals with us on anything that would destabilize us in a transition. He moves us to a place of stabilization on the inside before He moves us into something new on the outside. In this way, we discover transition isn't just about where you live or what you do. It begins with what is on the inside of you. He is taking you and me from strength to strength, from faith to faith, from glory to glory. (See Psalms 84:7, Romans 1:17.)

> *And we all, with unveiled face, beholding the glory of the Lord, are being transformed into the same image from one degree of glory to another. For this comes from the Lord who is the Spirit.* (Corinthians 3:18 EST)

Jesus stands at the threshold of every transition in life, with a crown over all other authorities and a voice above the crowd, saying, "Follow Me!" So we learn that we go through transitions in life because they are necessary for progress on the path of destiny.

Transitions Bring Us...

1. New Territory

The prophet Jeremiah shares God's Word about a coming time of transition that will change our narrative or the story we tell:

> Behold, the days are coming, declares the LORD, when they shall no longer say, "As the LORD lives who brought up the people of Israel out of the land of Egypt," but "As the LORD lives who brought up and led the offspring of the house of Israel out...[from] where he had driven them." Then they shall dwell in their own land.   (Jeremiah 23:7–8 ESV)

The purpose for the transition is always the same: to bring you into your divine destiny. Each time it happens, we come into a new place of influence to effect change. You step into new places you were destined to be in for kingdom purpose. It is important to recognize that places, positions, and even geographical locations are attached to your destiny. There are cities you are called to be in. God has given you these places, so you must transition if you are going to come into what has been prepared for you.

When you do, your story changes. What you know of God and have to say about Him spins out from what He has walked you through. Coming into new territory at the leading of the Spirit of God and into a new place of influence demonstrates God's immense ability to do the supernatural in our lives. It makes us a witness to how we got to where we are, which is all by His grace.

2. New Thinking

The mere word "transition" points to leaving something behind and moving into something new. To some degree, leaving things behind is a perpetual cycle in our lives.

Paul talked about it in Philippians 3:13: "One thing I do: forgetting what lies behind and straining forward to what lies ahead" (ESV). This gives us the mentality of transition, encouraging us to think a certain way—in a new way. This way of thinking is paramount to a life of destiny. We are meant to build upon what we know right now and God desires to bring creativity through us in ways that expand our capacity. This means we have to be willing to leave behind some old paradigms while holding on to our lasting principles so we can transition into new ways of thinking, creating new opportunity and momentum. Thinking differently leads to doing things in different ways and expanding your capacity in life. Taking the limits off in our thinking creates possibilities that can soon become reality but it all starts with new thinking. Allowing the Spirit of God to help you to think in new ways, higher ways, from a greater place of wisdom, will propel you into things you never dreamed possible, all because of how you think. Stay sensitive to the Spirit of God expanding how you think as you go through seasons of transition.

3. New Functioning

"Each new level in your life will require a new you." The point of this popular saying is that each new experience requires something different from us. It may be something completely different than what you've done in the past, so you need to develop a new way of functioning. Transitions ensure that this happens and require us to continue to mature into our full potential. It can feel awkward and uncomfortable because it is new to you, but don't let this deter you. God is forming a new functioning through you that brings about something more than what you have walked in before.

In the first book of Samuel, the Word of God talks about the Spirit of the Lord coming upon you and changing you into another person. (See 1 Samuel 10:6.) It goes on to say, *"Once this is fulfilled…do whatever your hands find to do, for God is with you"* (1 Samuel 10:7 MSG). In other words, although a new place will require you to function in a new way, jump into it with both hands and know God is with you.

So now that we have talked about some of the reasons why transition is necessary, I'd like to share three things I have learned that have stabilized me through seasons of transition.

Stay Close to Your Wells

You are going to need to drink deeply from the wells God has placed in your life—your own personal time with God. Transition is usually easy for worshippers because change is easiest in His presence. Stick close to the well of worship. In addition to your own set-aside time for worshipping

God, it's a good idea to play worship music in your home and your car. Stay close to the well of the Word of God in your life. And yes, this means time reading the Bible. Let Jesus reveal the Word to you. Meditate on it. Drink deep and let it go deep. And lastly, attend your church. This is no time to become a church skipper. You need what's in the well of your church and you need to sit under the ministry of your pastor to make your transition successfully.

Failing to stay close to your wells usually plays out in one of two ways. People either numb out, go shallow, and run from decisions, or they over-think and overanalyze until they are lost in total confusion. Both scenarios inevitably produce a prolonged season of transition and will throw one's destiny into a holding pattern. So make a quality decision that you are going to stay close to the wells of living water to keep your life on track.

Time Will Tell

A transition isn't just about going from one thing to the next. It's also about the process. God always uses the process of transition to reconstruct things in us. This is key because it sets us up for success in whatever God is moving us into. There can be a time to hold up before God in prayer when you sense something new is coming in your heart. There is a time when you begin to process and share what you are sensing with trusted people in your life, those with godly wisdom who will help you walk out the process.

And eventually, there is a time to act on what you know, leave some things behind, and press forward to the mark. This takes a Spirit-led finesse to protect you in the process. I can't stress this strongly enough: give the element of time its due diligence and let the burden of proof of your season of transition rest on God and His ability to make it clear and carry you through.

Guard Duty

Get your guard up! As the Lord spoke to my heart that day sitting in traffic, "Most accidents happen in places of transition." This is a time when you need to take guard duty on your thoughts and your words. Frustration levels can have a tendency to run high when you are heading into transi-tion. I have watched a lot of people allow frustration to translate into their focus on everything that's wrong with everyone and everything around them. But this would be a mistake. Let patience have her perfect work and in the meantime, stay steady.

Finally, who is truly ever ready to turn their life upside down and head into the unknown? And yet, for men and women of destiny, there is a part of us that yearns for this. We yearn for God to move us into something we cannot see but has destiny all around it. We live with the sense that we were created for it. If you can adjust your emotional gauge to align with your innate desire to feel destiny beneath your footsteps, your seasons of destiny will breed the perfect plan of God for your life.

If you are in a place of transition right now, let me pray this prayer over you.

Father, I pray over this one who is living out a season of transition of believing and seeking You for where they are to stay and where they are to move. For all that lies before them, I declare that they will see and know by the Spirit of the Lord, if and when and where they are to go. It is You who causes us to fulfill Your divine purpose for our lives. I thank you, Father, that right now, You cause their hearts to come to wisdom according to Psalm 90 and that Holy Spirit, You will comfort their soul in the process. God, You are our source and so we say together, our eyes are on You. In the name of Your Son, Jesus, Amen.

Questions to Reflect on:

Why would most accidents in life happen in seasons of transition?

_____

_____

_____

_____

_____

_____

_____

_____

_____

How should you respond if you find a truth unsettling?

_____

_____

_____

_____

_____

_____

_____

_____

_____

What happens when we put our faith in things of this world rather than God?

What are some helpful ways to deal with seasons of transition?

CHAPTER 5

THE CONTENDER

A contender is defined as someone who competes with another. Their goal is to take something that belongs to you. Contenders go after the title, the position, the prestige, the influence, or the power. What makes them very dangerous is the fact that a contender only goes after what belongs to another.

> **A CONTENDER ONLY GOES AFTER WHAT BELONGS TO ANOTHER.**

As a person of destiny, you have to be awake to the fact that a spiritual warfare is still going on over you to keep you out of your destiny. Although it is unseen to our natural eyes, you may sense it or feel the intensity of it at some times more than others. It can feel like you are in a wrestling match throughout the day with an unseen opponent. It can mess with you mentally because you might not even know why you have this sense of being in an unseen struggle, but you feel the effects of it. It can be wearing and very taxing on your energy. In the realm of the spirit, there are powers that contend with you for your place and portion in life. These powers are sent to stop, delay, withhold, or suspend the plan of God for your life. They know a person of destiny is a powerful force of change in the world.

The power of the right person in the right place is astounding. They are change agents and they bring an almost unstoppable dynamic. Your destiny is just that: God bringing you into the place He has called you to, for the purpose of bringing His goodness to a new level of prominence.

The Enemy Can Influence Anyone

Contenders try to keep you blocked out of your place, even in the physical realm. Influenced by the kingdom of darkness, even unknowingly, they can confront and openly challenge men and women of God, trying to take away what God has appointed as ours. This does not make them demonically possessed or even controlled, but any of us can be influenced and choose to yield to satan's agenda.

Let's look at a few examples found in the Word of God that give us precedent for when assignments from the kingdom of darkness are launched to keep men and women of God from coming into their divine place. If you look and listen with fresh eyes and ears, you can learn from them how to identity and overcome all that contends with you! In the book of Daniel, he writes about a fierce contention in the Spirit over his divine assignment.

> *But the prince of the kingdom of Persia withstood me twenty-one days; and behold, Michael, one of the chief princes, came to help me.*
> (Daniel 10:13)

The confrontation between the angel sent to assist Daniel and the Persian angel of darkness happened because Daniel connected with God through his prayers.

> *Then he said to me, "Fear not, Daniel, for from the first day that you set your heart to understand and humbled yourself before your God, your words have been heard, and I have come because of your words."*
> (Daniel 10:12 ESV)

Daniel was appointed to be in that city in that nation at that time, with position and influence to shift things—and there was a battle to keep him from it!

Another instance is found in the book of Esther. As a woman of destiny, she had quite a season of contention that was trying to get her out of her seat of authority by having her killed, along with all of the other Jews. Leading up to this, the enemy of her soul had been contending with her for over six years while she was queen. She was slowly influenced to shrink back in herself and merely "go with the flow." She became a product of her environment, hiding her true identity and never walking in the truth of who God had made her to be. Her hiding had started to become her defining.

Before we shake our head at Esther, let's ask ourselves this: Have you ever felt bombarded by thoughts or feelings of disillusionment? Maybe you were once feeling secure about your set place, but now, you're in a new season and you're not so confident, you're feeling disenfranchised, deprived of a right or privilege. A contender deprives you of revelation knowledge of who you are, what you are, and where you are called to be.

Just because you are faced with a bombardment of those thoughts and feelings doesn't mean they have to win. In chapter four of the book of Esther, we find out Esther spent three days in prayer and fasting. Somewhere in the stillness of this time, God regained the ground in Esther that she had lost. He visited with her and reminded the heart of this Hebrew woman, now in this key national position, that she didn't need a king to keep her, but I Am That I Am would keep her. All that she truly was came flooding back into Esther's heart—she was born of those who overcome! Armed with destiny, she overcame all that was contending with her and also out-strategized the contender of the whole Jewish race. They were saved that day, from the initial verdict of being destroyed. When it was all said and done, they were placed in a more prominent place in society. Esther's own uncle, Mordecai, who was also a Jew, was made counselor to the king.

> YOU HAVE AN ENEMY AND YOUR ONLY WAY THROUGH IS BY WHAT YOU CAN SENSE.

Whatever has come to contend with you, know that it is not just about you but about all that you will affect standing in the place God is readying for you. Don't get sidetracked by feelings and emotions of insecurity. Recognize that you have an enemy and your only way through is not by what you can see but by what you can sense. Because you have the Spirit of truth inside you, He is leading you in very calculated steps toward your destined place. You are in the seat of authority! Walk in it boldly! Take your cues from Him. This is *your* destiny. No one else but you can rise up and go after it. Refuse to be moved by what comes to oppose you. You have been given the Name that is above all Names and you have the rightful authority to use it and see God make the way. Remember Jesus's name can do anything He can do. And He has given you and me His Name to use.

Recognize Signs of the Enemy

So how do you know you are dealing with something influenced by the enemy to contend with you? Here are a few telltale indicators:

+ It burns with envy and jealousy.
+ It steals credit, affirmation, or position.
+ It practices competition and rivalry.
+ It despises the success of others.
+ It wrestles to find contentment.
+ It is aggressive.
+ It has a bitter tongue.

Remember, this can manifest in the spiritual and the physical realms. The spirit behind it seeks to kill, steal, and destroy. That is the mode of operation of that kingdom.

> ANYONE WHOSE GUARD IS DOWN CAN FALL PREY
> TO THE KINGDOM OF DARKNESS.

It also runs rampant looking for opportunities to effectively work against men and women of God. Anyone whose guard is down can fall prey to it. This does not make that person evil, just a pawn of the kingdom of darkness in that moment. If you experience this sense of rivalry coming at you on the path of destiny, rather than confront it, I would encourage you to take it to God in prayer. Bring the situation into the throne room of heaven, where heaven can silence it on your behalf in the realm of the spirit. If it persists, then ask the Lord to show you the strategy for coming through.

As believers, we must aggressively be on our guard. Contention can slyly slip in and become an attitude of the heart, so we don't realize we're being influenced by a spirit of darkness. The Word of God tells us not to be *"outwitted by Satan* [or] *ignorant of his designs"* (2 Corinthians 2:11 ESV). I believe this means we need revelation and discernment on which devices the enemy is using and when.

At certain times, you can look back and see how the enemy was using a particular assault at a specific time in your life for a reason. It was an appointed time and he wanted to try to shift it. But if we are aware and not ignorant of what and how he is attempting to gain footing, we will see it coming and stop it before it even begins. Contention is a particular way the enemy attempts to keep the body of Christ and believers out of their God-ordained places of assignment. I can almost pinpoint exact times in my own life and ministry over the past year where this has been the case.

The Enemy's Attacks Can Be Obvious

One occasion when this happened was so obvious and overt, it was shocking. I was in Niceville, Florida, on a Sunday morning, ministering at a great church there. After the service, I went to lunch with the pastors, then headed to the airport. I was flying to Tulsa, Oklahoma, to minister at an international leadership conference on Monday morning. I arrived at the airport a little late and was in such a rush to get checked in, I made a rookie mistake: I put my notes and Bible in my checked luggage, rather than in a carry-on. When you are in the traveling ministry and you are flying to speak at a meeting, you learn to never stick anything necessary in your checked luggage—specifically your Bible and your notes!

Once I had checked in, I headed for the gate, where I learned the flight was delayed due to storms. After we finally boarded the plane and it pulled back from the gate, as is typical in Florida, another storm rushed in. The lightning began and kept us grounded and unable to take off for two hours.

By the time I landed at my connecting airport in Dallas, it was almost midnight and I had missed the last flight out to Tulsa. The gate agent checked and told me there were no available seats on the morning flight to get me into Tulsa on time. At that moment, I knew I had a decision to make. Was this an attempt to contend with me to keep me from my divine appointment? Or was this simply something out of my control and I should kick back and go with the flow?

I had the strong sense that this was something contending with me to keep me from my destiny. I texted the leader in charge of the conference and she felt the same way. I made the decision I was not going to be pushed back. I went and got a rental car. I was ready to keep pressing onward, without my luggage. That meant no fresh clothes, no makeup, no notes, and no Bible. I started driving from the Dallas/Fort Worth airport toward Tulsa. By this time, it was close to 12:30 a.m. Around 2:45 a.m., I was getting sleepy and knew it wasn't a good idea to be driving any longer. I got off at the next exit and checked into a hotel room to sleep. My session was at 10 a.m., which meant I could only sleep for about three hours maximum if I was going to make it. Falling into bed in the same clothes I had ministered in that morning, I slept for exactly three hours. Back on the road headed toward Tulsa, I was calculating my time and knew it was going to be down to the wire.

When I reached Oklahoma City and came through to the north side, I knew I was in the home stretch. The Will Rogers Turnpike, just up ahead, would take me right into the city of Tulsa. As I got closer, I suddenly saw a serious situation ahead of me. There was a swarm of police cars blocking off the exit for the turnpike. A tractor-trailer was stuck and partially jackknifed under the exit overpass. Police were directing traffic off the highway and onto a local state route. I have driven that route from Oklahoma City to Tulsa at least a hundred times and have never seen a truck lodged under that overpass. I grabbed my phone to map an alternate route.

My thoughts turned to the service where I was about to minister and all the time it was taking me to get there. I knew instinctively that this must be important. Whatever God wanted to do in this service was being contended over. I was feeling the effects of what I had been through and thought, "I need to use this time I have left to pray and get ready for this service." I began praying in the Spirit out loud in the car. After just a few minutes of prayer, I heard the Lord speak to my heart: "Stop praying." I thought to myself, "Well, that is a strange thing to hear the Lord say to me. That must be me." Then He said, "Conserve your energy. Get out your phone, turn your voice memo recorder on, and I will dictate to you the service."

Wow. Everything on the inside of me got very serious. I grabbed my phone, did what He instructed, and quietly began to listen to my heart. Never in my life or ministry leading up to that point had I experienced the Lord dictating a message to me, one line at a time, like He did that day. The presence of God in my car got stronger and stronger. At this point, I was just a few miles from the end of the state route. Soon, I would be on the turnpike and driving into Tulsa. I kept an eye on the clock, knowing I had precious few minutes to spare.

I slowed down as I approached a railroad crossing in the middle of nowhere. Right at that moment, the lights lit up at the crossing—a train was coming. At a crawl. With grass growing over the railroad ties, I doubted many trains went through there.

At that point, I burst out laughing. I thought, "It is literally taking planes, trains, and automobiles to try and keep me from getting to my appointed place! But there is no way I am going to be stopped!"

I laughed the whole time all of those train cars crept by me at a snail's pace. "How obvious can you get, devil!?" I scoffed aloud.

When you are a messenger, your job is to deliver a message. You don't quit until you get the job done. I was determined. I knew in my heart I was supposed to be at the conference and I was going to keep going and press through.

While waiting for the train to pass, a valuable piece of information came to my attention. I was going to need gas to make it to Tulsa. When the tracks were finally clear, I saw a gas station just up ahead—the only gas station around. I jumped out in a flash, put my credit card in, and hit the button. The gas pump started...then came to a complete stop within seconds. I pulled the nozzle out and started it again. Nothing. After three attempts, I ran inside to tell the attendant what was happening and he came out to look at it. After just a couple of tries, he looked at me, perplexed.

"Ma'am, I have never seen our pumps do this and I have worked here a long time," he said.

This was getting nuts! I went into my purse, grabbed a $20 bill, and gave it to him. "Sir, I am in an extreme hurry," I said. "Would you go inside and turn this other pump on over there and I'll pull over there and use it?" He took off running and in a few minutes, my car finally had gas and I got back on the road.

With each place of contention, the sense of purpose I had only increased. The more you identify the contention around you, the easier it becomes to have a laser-like focus and determination to overcome it, by faith. If you do not know what you're fighting, then you cannot defend your position.

> ## IF YOU DO NOT KNOW WHAT YOU'RE FIGHTING, THEN YOU CANNOT DEFEND YOUR POSITION.

I pulled in front of the auditorium with three minutes to spare. Still in the clothes I had put on the day before in Niceville, Florida, I walked in and they took me straight to the green room. I will always be grateful for the lady who was waiting there with a case of makeup! She did her best to fix me up and they took me into the meeting. There was a quick introduction and they turned the service over to me.

Standing in front of these leaders who had come from all over the world—not just the United States but Europe, India, and elsewhere—I felt the overwhelming sense of destiny and the weight of the moment that had taken so much to reach. I knew the enemy had tried very hard to contend with me to keep me out of this place, but here I was and now the rest was dependent upon the anointing and yielding to Him. With no notes, only those that God had dictated to me on my phone and a Bible that my assistant had brought to me, I bowed my head and prayed over the Word. Prior to that day, I had never ministered with such clarity and direct understanding of what God wanted to say.

I was totally unaware of any fatigue from the almost non-stop pace of travel that I had just come through, or that I was running on barely three hours of sleep! I shared with the leaders about the plane, delays, the lodged tractor-trailer, the road closures, the phantom train, and the unprecedented gas pump debacle. I told them I knew God had some things He wanted to say to us and He was making the way for every place of destiny He had called us to, no matter what contended with us to attempt to keep us from them.

When my message was over, I prayed over the leaders present and turned the service back over to the emcee. As soon as it was over, the gentleman in front of me, who was also there speaking at the conference, turned around and looked at me. He said, "That was a message that the whole body of Christ needs to hear. If you ever get it recorded, I would like to broadcast it on my television network." The message the Lord had given me that day was on Joel's prophecy and the power of generational synergy. That story of contention is a very physical example of how much the enemy will work to try to keep you from your assignments.

Let's take a closer look at exactly how this work of contention can try to get its hooks into us. If we understand how this can occur, we can deal with it swiftly and stop it before it begins.

In the current climate of our culture, comparison, competition, and contention try to run wild, dominating large portions of our society. The chief contender has a cycle he uses to try to keep you out of your place and take it for himself. The cycle goes something like this:

Compare ⟶ *Compete* ⟶ *Contend*

Because it is so prevalent in our culture, it can be quite easy to find yourself falling under its influence. It can begin ever so slightly, with thoughts of comparison. If left unchecked, these grow into an attitude of competition. The next thing you know, you find yourself being heavily influenced by a spirit of contention.

Believers Must Not Be Contenders

Let me be clear: As believers, we are never to be in a place of contention with one another. Remember what contenders do: they go after what belongs to another. You and I have no business being concerned, even for one minute, with what belongs to another or what has been appointed for someone else. Someone else's place of influence, position, or assignment has nothing to do with your path of destiny and the calling God has prepared for you.

In my training for leaders, I like to put it to this way: "Your doors are your doors. Your divine place is your divine place. There is no need for you to contend for what is set up for another."

We are not supposed to be spending our time contending. We are called to spend our time possessing!

Right now, if you find yourself in the place where you realize that maybe you have had an attitude of comparison or competition, or you've even been contending with someone else, there is good news for you. If you are willing to do an honest soul search about how this attitude has been influencing your private thoughts, motives, or actions, then this is a clear sign your heart is reaching for truth. So, freedom from having anything to do with that junk is here for you.

Religiosity may tell you not to ever admit, even to yourself, that you have fallen short, but that is a lie—and it's a lie meant to rob you of the grace of God available to shift you and change you. I would just say, "Go and bring your heart before the Lord." Let the Lord speak to you and if you need to ask the forgiveness of someone who has felt the brunt of that previous attitude you were functioning in, then make it right. It is never too late to do the right thing and God will honor you for it.

IT IS NEVER TOO LATE TO DO THE RIGHT THING AND GOD WILL HONOR YOU FOR IT.

Moving forward, let's be sure to keep our hearts clear. I never want to be one who the enemy is able to use to cut down, delay, or detract from another. And the truth is, unless we are purposeful about it, it can happen to any of us. When I don't keep my spirit strong and rich in the Word of God, my flesh is susceptible to all kinds of ugly behavior that does not line up with my heart. Attitudes can take hold and damaging words can be said when all the while, our hearts are to see those around us flourish and be successful. This is motivation enough to stay strong in the Word, to ensure that God dwells richly in us.

We also have be aware that these things can come at *us*, shots fired from those close to us. In those moments, we have the opportunity to stand in judgment or release forgiveness and give mercy. Too many times, good relationships are lost because of a forever judgment made about a moment of weakness rather than years of relationship.

GOD EXPOSES THE ENEMY'S PLANS SO YOU CAN USE YOUR AUTHORITY.

Lastly, if you have felt yourself in a battle of contention, like you are in a wrestling match with an unseen opponent, God is opening your eyes to see what has really been going on so you can address it. He exposes the enemy's plans so you can use your authority. Let those who have contended with you contend no more. I have learned that when I recognize the enemy is specifically trying to contend with me to keep me out of my place, I get the advantage on him by spending focused time in the presence of God and listening to His Spirit within me. God will always show you how to outstrip your enemy, but we need to do things His way. When things come up that look like delays, instead of getting mad, go high and choose to stay in joy. Just like I had to laugh at that train! You keep hold of your faith in the truth that it is God who has appointed you and nothing can remove you from your set place as long as you don't quit.

I encourage you to declare this with a boldness out loud over yourself and your family:

I declare boldly that Jesus has already made me the one who always overcomes! I declare that no weapon that is formed against me shall prosper and all those who rise up against me shall fall. I declare that every lying word spoken about me falls to the ground and will not take shape, and that although many are the adversaries of the righteous, the Lord shall deliver me out of them all. I declare that power is in my hands to heal, to produce, to multiply, and to bless! And that authority has been given unto me by Jesus, my Lord. I declare that although hell may know my name, heaven has my back! I am fully supplied in every good work and I lack nothing in Jesus's Name. Amen and so be it unto me! As for me and my house, we shall serve the Lord!

Questions to Reflect on:

Why should people of God avoid contending with one another?

_____

_____

_____

_____

_____

_____

_____

_____

_____

What lesson can we learn from the book of Esther?

_____

_____

_____

_____

_____

_____

_____

_____

_____

_____

How can we recognize signs of the enemy?

What is the best way to deal with contention?

CHAPTER 6

THE ANCHOR FOR YOUR SOUL

Although we are far from perfect, I have been blessed with a very close family. We care for each other, pray for each other, and genuinely love one another. Having this background and being groomed and prepared for life in such a way set me up with a sort of intravenous solution of confidence and strength. Maybe it came from knowing I didn't stand alone or maybe it was because my foundations of self-esteem, spiritual connection, and purpose were solid. Most likely, it was all of the above.

I have many friends, however, who didn't grow up in the same family environment I've just described. Either one or both parents were missing or too immature and undeveloped in their ability to be a parent to provide what was needed. But in each of my friends' lives, somewhere along their path, they surrendered to God and He brought to them what they needed. He made up the difference so they could continue to grow and mature into healthy men and women of God.

For some, this came in the form of individuals who stood in the place of parents. I don't think we can overestimate the power of someone who steps in as a voice of wisdom, love, guidance, and even correction in people's lives. It is, in fact, a place of ministry all on its own. To be something they never had and give them what they need—wow! The ramifications of that in someone's life are exponential! And what a great need we have for people like this today.

If you are in your later years and are looking for purpose, for ways God can use you, may I just say that you are needed in our current society more than any other generation? In a culture largely comprised of children with absent fathers, absent mothers, and growing up in a gender confused age, you carry answers and a perspective that most of the Millennial and Z generations are searching for. Just the act of opening up some room for them with your attention, care, and listening ear creates a place for them to gain from you what they lack: a mother's or father's voice to validate, instill, inspire, and impart. It's more valuable than gold because it can't be bought.

In the culture of heaven, we are not defined by our origins but by our destination. The fabric of destiny can be woven in a person's life in a million different ways, thanks to the work of restoration that God delights in doing. It can bring wholeness to those who feel like they are fragmented and without a compass in life. This is what God specializes in. He secures our soul in every way while at the same time giving us wings to fly. When it happens in just one life, it is a piece that is added to the tapestry of legacy God is weaving, stretching all across eternity. He has been working it out before us and through us. If we but follow Him, it will stretch out beyond us.

Soul Security Is a Decision

Who among us has fallen short of the glory of God? All of us! None of us arrive entirely whole, healthy, mature, or as the Bible states, *"to the measure of the stature of the fullness of Christ"* (Ephesians 4:13). Though He lives within us, there is a process to this journey of being "in Him." It has been fully and freely given, but we have to choose to come into that supply of grace in our words, actions, character, and thinking. Oh, how we need His grace to do it! And in His grace is where we stand. Every day and all day, we choose with every step, every thought, and every word. We stand in the grace of God. These points of decision and choice cause me to grow into all God designed me to be. If I am not feeling the ebb and flow, the tension and release, of these choice dynamics in my daily life, then I am not growing. Situations come up and maybe I'm just letting my circumstances dictate my direction. Or worse yet, maybe I'm allowing my past behaviors and attitudes to call the shots. If this is the case, then I have caused myself to get stuck in a repetitive cycle of my own history repeating itself.

To be honest with you, I watch a lot of people get stuck in that cycle. They want to mature and grow, but they are unwilling to confront their own history of choices, decisions, and behaviors to actually grow and mature on the path of destiny.

We are innately made to protect and secure ourselves as human beings. We instinctively pull back the part of us that is hurt to protect and soothe it. For instance, there is nothing normal about putting yourself in harm's way to protect another—it goes against every human tendency we have—and yet there are brave men and women who do this every day. We are programmed to protect and secure ourselves. This built-in sense of self-preservation works to secure our basic needs of survival: air, water, food, warmth, and rest.

Our soul does the same thing. It needs to feel secure. Over time, our humanity will develop ways to make sure our soul feels secure and protected. These are developed in large part based on our past experiences and the environments we have been exposed to. Out of these felt needs, the soul looks to attach to something secure and places demands on our will to meet these needs.

It is interesting to notice all of the ways your soul, left on its own, can develop to try to provide security for itself. What seems like merely seeking comfort for your soul can actually come from an unhealthy place, be harmful to your life, and destructive to your destiny. It may satiate a momentary desire, but it can cripple you. It will take away from you rather than add to you. What your soul thinks it needs in order to feel secure could actually be your kryptonite. Like the radioactive substance that weakened Superman, it could be your weakness, your Achilles' heel.

> ### WHAT YOUR SOUL THINKS IT NEEDS IN ORDER TO FEEL SECURE COULD ACTUALLY BE YOUR KRYPTONITE.

We need to be aware of some unhealthy attempts at soul security, such as attachments to people in an attempt to satiate a need for approval. We may seek out relationships with the opposite sex, peers, authority figures, or a parental figure, all in pursuit of attaining a level of acceptance. It's as though we were on an unseen and unspoken quest to be able to tell ourselves, "I am secure because I am enough in the eyes of this person."

Sometimes, soul security can come from food attachments, drinking attachments, or a constant need to obtain high-value status symbols or material items. The goal of marketers and merchandisers today is not to produce enough to satisfy the cravings of human nature but to enlarge the appetites of the masses to consume an enormous number of products. This plays into humanity's attempts to secure its own soul, to use the status of owning material things to *"live and move and have our being"* (Acts 17:28), rather than the Lord.

Material possessions and the need for them in order to secure status becomes a tyranny over us in several ways. We become expert hunters rather than users, with status symbols becoming trophies to show our value to the outside world. It is a dangerous game of accumulation and soul deception and let me tell you now, it has no end. We pile up "stuff" throughout our life without gaining any value of life. As a result, we begin to undervalue spiritual things. In an age obsessed with consuming clothes, cars, cell phones, and status symbols for the goal of impressing others, people's lives hang in the balance. Becoming a product of this environment enthrones our persona and the opinions of others in the place of Jesus. Yet after obtaining these things, we are no more deeply satisfied or possess any more true joy than we did before.

Immersing our souls in things that are unhealthy and living from this place impacts our spiritual senses. It dims the eyes of our heart, makes our experiences in the presence of God become vague and His voice hard to hear. It deadens our sensitivity to God and who He is. This whole pursuit of soul satisfaction only intensifies the need, enlarges the craving to consume, and deadens spiritual hunger for the true and just, the honest and the good. It becomes harder to concentrate on things that *"eye has not seen, nor ear heard"* (1 Corinthians 2:9), things God is revealing to us by His Spirit.

Neither people nor things can ever satisfy that yearning inside us, the need to feel complete. Nothing of this world is ever enough. It never lasts, it always wears off, and the craving, the hunt, the attempts to secure your soul's security begin once again.

There Is Only One Anchor for Our Souls

The answer is simple: the presence of God is the only real and true anchor for our souls. He is the one true King of our heart and only when He is seated there will you and I feel the gratification of knowing we are complete. Yes, there really is a soul gratification this side of heaven. It is so solid and satisfying that nothing can shake you from it. It is being in the presence of God, with His goodness and His love washing over you. Most of us need to be in His presence more than just for a little while to let Him saturate and fill us up completely.

Typically, in order to find your connection in His presence, you must be willing to let go of what you have been using to fix your soul's security issues. You need to leave behind the crowd you used to constantly check with to see if they applauded you and instead discover the deeper place of knowing God approves of you and how great His love for you really is.

> YOUR SOUL CANNOT STRENGTHEN ITSELF.

Yes, your soul is going to look for something to latch on to for strength. Your soul cannot strengthen itself—it needs to attach to something to be strong and secure. We were made to be connected to and in union with the One who loves us and can provide us with all we need. Problems arise when we search for soul attachments outside of Him.

> Woe to the rebellious children, says the Lord, Who take counsel, but not of Me, And who devise plans, but not of My Spirit, That they may add sin to sin. Who walk to go down to Egypt, And have not asked My advice, To strengthen themselves in the strength of Pharaoh, And to trust in the shadow of Egypt! (Isaiah 30:1–2)

You get the sense in these verses from Isaiah that this is very personal to God. His people have turned to something else for their security and protection when He put everything on the line for them. Everything else is so inferior to His strength and He loves us so intensely that it hurts Him when we turn to something else.

David Turned to God for Strength

In contrast to this, I want to share a story of genuine soul security with you and how to connect to the anchor of your soul. This story will also make it very obvious why the Word of God describes David as a man after God's own heart. (See Acts 13:22.)

This is a snapshot of how David learned to cope and satiate his own soul. This story comes on one of the worst days of his life. He and his men returned to their hometown to discover it had been attacked in their absence. The city was burned to the ground and all of their homes were gone. And the unimaginable had happened: their wives and children had been captured by the enemy army. David and his men *"lifted up their voices and wept, until they had no more power to weep....Now David was greatly distressed, for the people spoke of stoning him, because the soul of all the people was grieved, every man for his sons and his daughters"* (1 Samuel 30:4, 6).

This is where you see what is really in a person. What do you turn to for consolation at such a moment in life? Where do you look for strength for your soul?

But David strengthened himself in the Lord his God.

(1 Samuel 30:6)

David fastened upon the Lord. He reached out to God and God took hold of David. The Word tells us that He strengthened, aided, helped, repaired, recovered, and fortified David in his soul.

God wants to do this for you as well. And in reality, only He can do it. On your very worst day, by His love and grace, God still sees the very best of you and pulls you through anything you and I will ever face.

Even the best of us still need an anchor for our soul. David, as strong as he was, knew he needed something to lift his soul somewhere.

To You, O Lord, I lift up my soul. (Psalm 25:1)

This hope we have as an anchor of the soul, both sure and steadfast, and which enters the Presence behind the veil. (Hebrews 6:19)

Love inoculates you. It cuts off thoughts and feelings that you are anything less than enough, capable, worthy, and chosen for everything God has called you to.

This Love, the love of the Father, breaks through past experiences based in fear and rejection; it frees you to believe all things are possible. You are so loved, cherished, and believed in by all of heaven because the Father of creation decided upon you and decided to set His love on you. His love will make you solid from the inside out and be your contentment.

BEFORE YOU COULD EVER CHOOSE HIM, HE CHOSE YOU FIRST.

Every time I lift my soul to the Lord, I am building the destiny God designed for me, with each decision of every day. Remember this: before you could ever choose Him, He chose you first. He loved you first. He didn't wait to see what you would do and then set His love on you. He was all-in for you before you ever decided on Him. A love like this cannot be matched. Sometimes, I find myself thinking about how God did that for me and it inspires me to believe Him and receive from Him more and more.

God Is with You All the Time

Thinking about His love and reading it in the Bible has also brought a new level of closeness to Him in my everyday life. I love it that there is always more of God to experience and He is with me all the time. The reality is this: feeling the presence of God with you and close to you all the time can become as literal as you make room for. If you make it a habit to pause and recognize His presence with you, He will become more of a reality to you wherever you are. Your soul will experience the security you need in a more tangible way. You will believe in Him and receive Him in your heart. The Spirit of God as the anchor for your soul means you have everything you need all of the time at your disposal.

If love inoculates me from fear and sets me free, then I choose the One who chose me first. You can put your trust in Him every time. He never lets go, He never looks back to second-guess anything about you. He causes you to see and know everything you need to see and know. He is the One who has your back when everyone else has left.

> ## GOD IS THE ONE WHO HAS YOUR BACK
> ## WHEN EVERYONE ELSE HAS LEFT.

He has never flinched in your defense or care. He has carried you when you didn't know you had lost strength. He got you through when you didn't know which way to go or where to move. When we come to Him, He always has room. He has not changed and He never will. To decide to follow Him and His lead is the simplest yet greatest road we could travel on. He has shown us time and time again that nothing is impossible when we make Him our anchor, our go-to. He doesn't want to be honored in your life—He wants to be the supply in your life.

A dear friend of mine who is a gifted songwriter wrote a song that speaks so clearly to building your realization of God's goodness toward you and trusting in Him.

"Faithful" by ReJeanna Jolliff

When the sun is shining
When the storms are raging
I know You are Faithful
Always there to guide me
In Your strength you hide me
I know You are Faithful.
In the morning Your mercy greets me
As I walk Your grace it covers me
Through my nights and all my days
I'll trust You Lord
You Are Faithful
I'm leaning on your arms of grace

Your love inspires my faith to believe
That you were always there
For I know You Are Faithful

Questions to Reflect on:

Why would heaven define us by our destination rather than our origins?

What sources of soul security do you have that might be unhealthy?

What made David a man after God's own heart?

_____

_____

_____

_____

_____

_____

_____

_____

_____

How can we better understand God's love for us?

_____

_____

_____

_____

_____

_____

_____

_____

_____

_____

CHAPTER 7

FAITH FOR YOUR DESTINY

There is a quote I have written down in a book I have kept for a long time now. It came from a woman who defied many odds to fulfill her divine destiny as a missionary to Brazil. It's her tenacity of faith that makes her words so powerful, even still today.

> "On the substance of things not seen, you and God can do anything. For all achievements are but dreams of faith carved into concrete."
> —Rosalee Mills

Faith for your destiny gives you the wings on which you can rise to fulfill the divine purpose for which God has given you vision. Christopher Columbus had new routes around the world in his vision long before he discovered the Americas. Harriet Beecher Stowe, with eyes of faith, saw her nation without slavery. David Livingstone could see a better Africa. John G. Lake could see beyond disease and by faith in God envisioned the skin of lepers as healed and made white as snow.

Jesus was the manifestation of the faith God has in a lost world. When a person fearlessly lays hold of faith and releases its power to fulfill their destiny, others can use this flame of faith to light their own lamp for their life's journey.

Faith is critical to destiny. Like a fish to water, they go hand in hand. If we ally ourselves to faith in God, then our lives will be in a constant state of progress, destiny realized, and an elevation to new heights. Each and every act of faith becomes a catalyst to a greater place of reigning in life. Living by faith becomes a daily enriching experience, just by living in obedience to God's word.

> ## EACH ACT OF FAITH BECOMES A CATALYST TO A GREATER PLACE OF REIGNING IN LIFE.

If we do not ally ourselves to faith, we go nowhere or drag ourselves down. And the further down we go, the more likely we are to keep losing ground.

Without faith it is impossible to please Him, for he who comes to God must believe that He is, and that He is a rewarder of those who diligently seek Him. (Hebrews 11:6)

What Jesus did on the cross in redeeming our lives freed us from all that was below us. He gave us the ability to live by the faith in Him, Jesus Christ!

The beauty of it is we do not stand alone. When we join forces in faith, we become a body of allies whose mission is to expand the kingdom of God. I don't know if we fully realize just yet how strong of a bond this is and what it can produce. We are the preserving force in the world, both salt and light. As the body of Christ, we have representatives in every country whose voices speak the Word of God in every tongue. Although it has been fought, ridiculed, censored, and imprisoned, it is the strongest, longest lasting coalition the world has yet known. Is there any other march through history that started with only One and has added millions of people to its ranks, from all ages and races, for more than 2,000 years?

Guard your heart and the voices you allow to speak to you about your alliance with your heritage of faith, which is the body of Christ where God has connected you, through your local church. I always cringe when I hear people talking about their local church and pastors in a sort of "over the top" way. They go on and on about how awesome it is, as if they have finally found "the place" that's doing it right. I cringe because I know they are under an illusion and they are headed for a stark wake-up call. The Christian church is not perfect and neither is any pastor, minister, leader, or staff. Every church has its challenges and every church is still working it out one step at a time. But as the body of Christ, we are called to love one another through the imperfections.

In his book, *An Unstoppable Force*, Pastor Erwin McManus writes:[9]

"The Christian community is not a place without interpersonal crisis or challenge…that's why biblical community (being a part of the local church) is such an extraordinary gift…When you begin to love people through their imperfections, through the disappointments, you begin to know that it's more than infatuation."

The enemy of your soul seeks for ways to cut you off from your place of connection. The church of Jesus Christ, the ecclesia, is and was His plan and is still the ascending force of the future. I believe God is raising up teams of people to join forces and who, by faith, will dramatically affect whole cities and even nations in our generation.

> ## EACH TIME WE USE OUR FAITH TO FULFILL A PLACE OF DIVINE DESTINY, IT PUTS GOD'S GLORY ON DISPLAY.

Each time we use our faith to fulfill a place of divine destiny, it puts God's glory on display. This is the manifestation of Christ in you, the hope of glory. By way of example, we see the glory of a free-roaming mustang when it's running at full gallop with all of its strength, doing what it was made to do. When you watch a beautiful mustang running, it's enough to stop you in your tracks. That is what it means to behold or see the horse's glory. In the same way, the glory of you is seen when you are doing exactly what you were designed to do in the way you were uniquely designed to do it.

Each and every step is going to require your faith.

---

9. Erwin McManus, *An Unstoppable Force: Daring to Become the Church God Had in Mind* (Loveland, CO: Group Publishing Inc., 2001)

The Great Collaboration of Destiny

Faith for your destiny involves more than just believing a divine destiny for your life exists. It is going to require the full expression of faith—believing it, speaking it, and acting on it, as the Spirit of God leads you. This is what separates those who actually fulfill their divine destiny from those who may sense they have one but never do anything about it.

If faith is what it takes, then understanding faith and how it works should have the full attention of a person of destiny. *"Faith is the substance of things hoped for, the evidence of things not seen"* (Hebrews 11:1 KJV).

As we've seen, destiny is a projected path—an intended, prepared plan, designed and laid out by your heavenly Father. It is waiting for you—and this is your faith comes in. God's bold blueprint that He designed for you, when combined with your faith, becomes the great collaboration of destiny being fulfilled in your life.

The Word of God tells us *"faith comes by hearing and hearing by the Word of God"* (Romans 10:17). So first and foremost, no matter what resources and tools we have to help us grow in knowledge, if they are not based on the Word of God, they will not tap into our faith, and thus cannot help us fulfill our destiny.

And now abide faith, hope, love...   (1 Corinthians 13:13)

So we know destiny requires our faith, but now we understand we need to add hope to our faith. Hope for your destiny is paramount because it fuels your passion and keeps your faith sharp, active, and alive. Hope keeps your faith looking for what it is believing. Hope is a powerful force; when people have hope, they are very hard to stop.

> HOPE FOR YOUR DESTINY FUELS YOUR PASSION AND KEEPS YOUR FAITH SHARP, ACTIVE, AND ALIVE.

One way a person without hope is defined is "lost." If those without hope are lost, then when we have hope, we are found—found right in the middle of God's plan.

Live Each Day Assuming Good Awaits

If you are a person of faith *and* a person of hope, you live each day from a place of assuming good is waiting for you and you are about to encounter it.

This is not a whimsical "fairy tale" hope but a hope based on a solid foundation of faith, on the evidence of things not seen. It is key to a life of destiny. If you are a person of faith and hope, you are perpetually expecting to experience destined moments, all the time. This is one of the highest ways you and I can live with God.

Paul said, *"For I know that this will turn out for my deliverance..."* (Philippians 1:19). He had the expectation that even when his current situation looked bad, faith and hope would save him. He was saying, "Even right now, God is working this into a good thing, a divine thing for me." You simply cannot stop a person of faith and hope.

The Rev. Cathy Mink, a powerful woman of God who has been in my life for some time, shared some things with me from her own life of faith. I tucked them away in my heart because I knew they were coming from real life experience. She and her husband have exemplified a life of faith to me for over twenty-five years. She said to me:

> "Faith takes hold of the promise of God with boldness, regardless of the current situation. It disregards everything that isn't in line with the promise and it never gives a crisis its respect. Faith isn't swayed by things that come up that look like bumps in the road because faith is a rest. It gives you supernatural abilities that go beyond your own strength."

These powerful truths have served as the standard for me each time I have come to a new place or season where I need to use my faith in a big way.

I have learned to first spend extra time with God. I simply let His love and presence wash over me. I do this before I do any praying, declaring, or decision-making. After bowing my head and listening with a quiet heart, I can then move toward using my faith with confidence and determination—not because of my own strength but because I am so very aware of how much God is with me, in me, and for me. The successful outcome is settled in my heart. I am seeing the end from the beginning, just like my Father.

Faith sees potential, then speaks and moves. Love knows that in the end, all of the glory goes to Him. If destiny is knocking on the door of your heart with some new things, you already have what it takes to achieve it. It's a seed inside you. All you need is to get into a place where it can germinate.

Get in the quiet room of the Spirit of God, where He can begin to develop the picture of what He has designated for your life. Let Him lead you by still waters and remind you of His goodness and His power. From there, begin to look and see with the eyes of faith. Remember that faith, hope, and love remove all of the limits and are not afraid to go big.

Are You Limiting God's Plans?

Recently, I was driving from Fort Worth, Texas, to Nashville, Tennessee. I typically fly for trips of that distance, but I had been spending so much time in airports and cooped up on airplanes that a drive seemed like a nice reprieve. I admit I was having second thoughts about four hours into my drive, but nonetheless, there I was! The nice thing about driving I have always enjoyed is that you can control your own atmosphere.

I had just finished listening to a friend's message about how God has clothed us in glory. He communicated it so well, it stirred me up. I was driving along, just thinking about all he had shared, when suddenly, God began to talk to me. He said, "You are limiting and delaying Me." Immediately, God had my attention. In my heart, I thought, "Lord, what do You mean? How?"

He spoke to me again, "With those things you are believing Me for." I said, "But Lord I am truly believing You for those things."

He replied, "Yes, you started out in faith believing Me, but then after you prayed and made your declaration, you started working out in your own head all the different ways you could see as possibilities of how it could happen. When you did that, you put the limits on Me. Now your faith has shifted from Me over to the ways YOU have contrived in your head it can come about. But I am not working in those ways. And until you let go of the how and get back to simply putting your faith in Me, you have shut Me down and I can't work."

In a flash, I could see everything He was talking to me about. I was doing exactly what He had described. There were some pressing needs for the ministry and in my own life that I had just begun to believe God for. Shortly after I made my declaration of faith, almost subconsciously, I began to think through all the ways I thought it could happen. I had started using my problem-solving skills to work out all of the ways I thought God could do it.

He said, "Many times, people start out believing Me and standing on My word, but then they stall and delay things I have been working on for them when they do this. Just stick with your part. Yours is the believing part. Mine is the doing part."

Driving along Interstate 40 that day, I came into a new place of understanding how to walk in faith for my destiny. I immediately made the adjustment. I said, "Lord, I see it and I am so grateful that You made this clear to me. Right now, I repent of trying to do Your part and problem-solve and put my faith in my version of how You can accomplish these things. I take my hands off of all of it and step back into my place of faith and trust in You and Your word that is solid and true. And I leave the rest of it to You."

In that moment, I felt an unexpected release come over me, a release from pressure and anxiety I didn't even know were there. I had weighed myself down trying to figure how God was going to do what I was believing Him to do and all the ways I thought were possible for Him to do it.

GOD HAS TRILLIONS OF WAYS TO BRING HIS WORD TO PASS AND "OPTIONS" ARE NOT AN ISSUE.

I learned a valuable lesson that day. God needs no precedent! He is not bound to working by anything He has ever done before or any previous way He has ever worked before. He has trillions of ways to bring His word to pass and "options" are not an issue for our God!

The feeling of relief and freedom that flooded me then was amazing. I drove down the highway laughing out loud, feeling so much joy from the truth that collaborating with God through faith would bring me to my destiny.

The very next day, I was going through the mail and came across an envelope from an organization I had not connected with in a couple of years. I almost threw it away, thinking it was probably just a general mailing letter but decided to open it instead.

It was a personal letter to me from the CEO, a man I had only met once but had very high respect for. He said our ministry had been in his thoughts for quite some time and enclosed an offering for $5,000 to be a blessing in our endeavors. Standing there in amazement, I heard the voice of the Holy Spirit. "I am always working to bring things to pass in ways you would never think of," He said.

Live by Faith to Partner with God

Living by faith is truly a partnership with God, and yet it's so important that we know which part is ours and let God do the rest so we don't limit His working for us!

Ask the Spirit of Truth to tell you what divine steps you are to take and what He wants you to do. And when He shows you, don't delay—move, act boldly and with excellence. Be confident. This is how you use your faith to fulfill your destiny. Each step is important and leads to the next. But walking this way, living this way, is what you were made for and how your calling is going to become your reality. It is the greatest adventure this side of heaven and one you do not want to miss!

There is something waiting for you that resonates so deeply in you that when you step into it, overwhelming truth rises up and says to you, "You were born for this." This is the essence of destiny. What you were born "for."

Even Jesus, when He walked the earth, repeatedly said the Father sent Him for a purpose. Destiny was speaking to Him—and destiny is speaking to you and me. It is the heartbeat of your Father when He conceived you in love and vision. He breathed your life into existence and in that breath was not just your being, your timing, your personality, your abilities, and your sensibilities but also the purpose for which you were sent.

The Father's breath included your divine destiny. Fulfilling this breath of God within you is the true meaning of your life.

The experiences of life teach us and train us, but they are not the purpose of life itself. Our purpose is to bring an experience or an influence into the world we have been placed in. Our purpose is to develop all that God has put in seed form within us so we can bring a force of our Father into the time that is ours to affect.

Watch those who are going somewhere on purpose. Something is driving them. There is something they feel compelled to accomplish.

What are you compelled to accomplish? Have you ever asked yourself that question before? The answer can shift, multiply, and mature, but it has to start somewhere.

Look for Moments of Decision

Let me share with you a few of those moments for me.

I was speaking at Cyril Assembly and there was a young woman in the crowd who had a call upon her life, but she was not living a life that looked anything like her destiny. She sat in the crowd with her shoulders slumped, but her eyes locked in. I could tell she hung on every word like it was a lifeline or her last chance. At the end of the service, she came to the front of the auditorium for prayer. She said she knew this was a big moment for her. As I prayed for her, the most overwhelming sense of destiny came over me. In that moment, I realized the biggest reason I was there, in that state, in that city, at that time, was to be there for this young woman in her moment of decision.

I looked at her and told her exactly what I knew to be true: "If for no other reason, I am here tonight for you." She broke down and began to cry. We prayed together and that moment served as a turning point for both her and her little daughter.

> THIS LIFE IS NOT ABOUT YOU OR
> HOW GOOD OF AN EXPERIENCE YOU CAN HAVE.

Moments like this make everything worthwhile. It reminds you that this life is not about you or how good of an experience you can have. It's about being there for someone else, to help them "become" or see what they need to see. It's about being a conduit for God for someone in a certain moment. It's the fulfillment of all that you long for on the inside.

Answering a Mandate from the Lord

Another moment for me was standing backstage at an event center in the island nation of Grenada. It was the opening night of our nationwide women's conference. It had taken a full year of work and preparation to host this international ministry event. It was the biggest undertaking for me and my team to date, and at times during that year, it looked like an impossibility. We started with nothing, but I knew I had heard from God. This was what He was asking me to do. It took so many others saying "yes" as we shared the vision for reaching the women of a nation that has been dishonored and broken in so many ways. In the end, it was one step of faith at a time. I witnessed miracle after miracle that year.

Doing an event like this in a small island nation is not like doing it in the United States. For instance, if you need something, you can't go to a Walmart to get it. I had a clear mandate from the Lord that this event was to be done first-class as a sign to these women that God was honoring what had been dishonored and restoring what had been broken. Our planning required us to think through every single detail of what we would need from start to finish. It had to be thought of, purchased, packed in shipping containers, shipped to Grenada, and then unpacked and set up. Just to put it in perspective, this would be like opening a mega-church overnight, running it with a group of people, most of whom had never met before, then tearing it down and shipping it home. In the natural, it is ridiculous to attempt—but the grace of God was upon us.

We brought in world-class musicians, singers, and artists. We rented the only LED screen on the island that stood over twenty feet tall to show videos of how God was championing the cause of women of destiny in the island nations. We were so honored to have the help and support of so many wonderful local pastors and their families, who became dear friends. The U.S. embassy charge d'affairs to Grenada was in attendance, along with his staff. The news media from across the island covered the event from beginning to end. The government of Grenada lent their full support, including the prime minister, with whom I was invited to meet, and every courtesy was extended to me and my team. The entire undertaking was unprecedented in every way. It took the tireless and dedicated work of my amazingly talented staff, leadership team, and a host of volunteers. In the end, it all came together in grand style. Watching the women arrive and walk the red carpet as our volunteers held up signs reading, "Welcome! You Made It!" and cheer and clap as they got registered was amazing to witness.

On opening night, I stood backstage, peeking out at the crowd, at all the women who had come as our first-class worship team and band led the charge. It felt like there was electricity in the air. I just stood there watching in awe. And I wept. I laughed. I jumped. And I cried. All of it at once! I had never felt such overwhelming emotion like that before. Tears of thankfulness and joy streamed down my face that the vision was coming to pass and women's lives were being changed by encountering God! It was all so much. That God had entrusted something so precious to me was astounding. And in that moment, right before I walked out on the stage, it came rushing up from my heart and filled every part of me: "This is what I was born for. I was born for this moment. This was a destined place for me and I am here."

Not every day is full of an "I was born for this" moment, but those moments fuel you for all the rest of the "in between" times. The Word of God tells us, *"Where there is no vision, the people perish"* (Proverbs 29:18 KJV). Sometimes, this is a slow, miserable perishing. But the opposite is also true: when people have vision and purpose, they flourish! Why would we want to live for anything else?

Questions to Reflect on:

Why do we need faith in order to reach our destiny and assume our calling?

_____

_____

_____

_____

_____

_____

_____

_____

_____

_____

_____

_____

How can we collaborate with destiny?

_____

_____

_____

_____

_____

_____

_____

_____

_____

In what ways have you cooperated with God's plans for you or limited them?

What happens when we live with purpose and vision?

CHAPTER 8

THE NEED FOR SPEED

A Massachusetts college professor once noted that someone living today receives more stimuli in twenty-four hours than anyone living a few generations ago received in their lifetime. Our environment drives us. It is constantly yelling for attention and demanding a response. And it never stops! Thanks to smart phones, twenty-four-hour news cycles, social media, text messaging, email, and a globally connected transient age, it is possible to be in motion and communication night and day. Although this has brought untold benefits and developments to the world, some things have been sacrificed in the midst of all of this activity.

The barrage of stimuli is everywhere. In fact, it has so saturated our way of life that most people are bouncing from one paid ad to the next for their information, entertainment, buying decisions, and even philosophy for life. Originality in imagination and creativity are replaced with a pre-fab, menu-driven mentality. Why bother spending time imagining or creating options on your own? In today's culture, we are groomed to simply choose from the predesigned menu options, rather than thinking about options that might exist that are not on the menu.

Time magazine reported:

"The average attention span for the notoriously ill-focused gold-fish is nine seconds, but according to a new study from Microsoft, humans now generally lose concentration after eight seconds, highlighting the affects that an increasingly digitalized lifestyle can have on the brain."[10]

In an age where anything to be known is a Google search away, it can be easy to forget that merely accumulating knowledge does not produce growth or progress on the path of your destiny.

Speeding through life, day in and day out, makes just enough time and space for what I call "surface impressions" of the sights and sounds you catch as you go speeding by. Recent polls have shown most people now get their news and current events from social media. In fact, after the 2016 U.S. presidential election, most of the voters who were polled said they based their decision on what they read and saw on social media. With the average online attention span of around eight seconds, it's jaw-dropping to think that, as a nation, many of us came to our conclusion about who to vote for as president through a series of eight-second social media visuals and sound bites.

WE ARE MOVING SO FAST, WE NOW PREFER TO CONSUME OUR INFORMATION VIA PICTURES.

To compound this situation, the majority of social media consumers are using image-driven platforms such as Instagram and Snapchat, which means we are moving so fast, we now prefer to consume our information via pictures. We substitute pictures for paragraphs, saving us the effort of having to read and think or use our imagination to picture something in our mind. Thus, in order to grab the attention of the masses to "say something," the tendency is to use sensationalism to make an impression. I think we all know how dangerous this has become in our culture. Because of this sensationalism, no one truly knows what to believe anymore.

Stimuli from the outside can only tattoo the surface of a person's life. In the need for speed, there is no way any genuine, rich, empowering deposits or values can be gained. We receive mindless attention-grabbers rather

10. http://time.com/3858309/attention-spans-goldfish

than worthwhile investments of truth-telling. When it comes to your spiritual growth and development as a person of destiny, our cultural environment becomes a real issue. The kingdom does not operate at break-neck speed—quite the opposite. Nor does heaven need sensationalism because it is the real deal. So to participate in the things of God's kingdom, you and I must be the real deal, too. The good news is heaven will wait for us to get to a place of genuine living.

I like to put it this way: Just because you get a tattoo of something "on you" does not prove you have something in you.

God Is Waiting to Speak to You

The depth of a person comes from the time they have taken to be in the presence of God, to listen to His still, small voice. The same God who split a sea, rained food for His people, and called a man to walk on water is in the room wherever you are, waiting to speak to your heart. But we do have to be still and quiet so the Spirit can reveal His truth to us, so it can become part of who we are. These are original source, organic deposits and impartations that dig out the well of our potential and begin to fill it with living water to fuel us with revelation, not just information. It is uniquely personal and intimate between you and God. It is not regurgitated leftovers from someone else's moment but your moment, raw with heaven's power and totally your own. This is so monumental on the path of destiny because once you own it, you have it to give. God has given us this invitation to spend time with Him and have these moments with Him that make indelible marks upon our life.

If I may say this to you, at this point of your journey, wherever you may be in life, make the decision to go fight for your moment. It's worth fighting for. Don't settle for only ever getting what's relayed from someone else's moment. Take what they give and then go find yours. Carve out your time and your place to be with God.

Pace Yourself for the Race

To be a person of destiny, I have to watch skillfully over my own internal pace. I can't afford to let this need for speed infiltrate it. If I do, I am no doubt sacrificing a great deal.

I recall a moment a few years ago that speaks to this. I had just arrived at the John F. Kennedy International Airport. I was speaking in the New York City area that weekend. As I was coming through security and heading toward the baggage claim area, I happened to notice, in the massive crowd, someone I knew who was walking toward me! What were the chances?! When I say I know this person, I mean we are close—as in talk a few times a week close! I knew she had also been in the area to speak somewhere, but I thought she had already left town. She was walking very fast and determined and as we walked toward each other, I broke into a big smile, waiting to greet my friend. Being just a few steps away from her now, I realized the look on her face did not match my own. In fact, she wasn't even looking at me—she was looking right past me, quite seriously. In that moment, I realized she didn't even see me! There I was, just steps away from her, someone she knows very well, and yet she didn't even realize I was standing right there. As she breezed past me, I finally blurted out her name. Her abrupt stop and look of shock is something we still laugh about. She was running late for a flight and clearly on a mission! It's amazing that you can be moving so fast that someone you know intimately can be so close to you and yet you are unaware.

I think this happens frequently to us when it comes to the kingdom of God.

There are things that drive us internally, even in our pursuit of fulfilling the will of God. Let's take a look at a word that isn't often attached to pursuing a life of destiny but comes into play more than we realize: ambition. Dictionary.com defines it as "an earnest desire for some type of achievement or distinction, as power, honor, fame, or wealth, and the willingness to strive for its attainment; the object, state, or result desired or sought after; desire for work or activity; energy."

The need to achieve is a silent problem among the leaders and emerging leaders of our day. Ambition is sneaky. It wears the cloak of mission and assignment but long absences from the still waters and quiet alone places with the lover of our soul can bend the great commission into mere self-ambition and putrefy the waters in our well.

"Better than speed of action is an accurate sense of direction."
—Ralph W. Sockman

Because the environment of our generation adjusts our minds to the headlines and quick one-liners that attempt to bottom-line spiritual truth, we have to dig our heels in to create an inner place of stillness where an appetite for knowing God can form. This is a real place cultivated in your private inner life. This isn't something you can do in a corporate setting, only in a quiet, solitary place.

WE HAVE TO DIG OUR HEELS IN TO CREATE AN INNER PLACE OF STILLNESS.

This place isn't about you, or the issues you currently face. Rather, it is about being in His presence and knowing it is enough. We need to press in to get to the place where we don't have to fight to be still but rather require it. You require interaction with Him. Yes, at first, you might have to wrestle yourself down from the knee-jerk reaction to the need for speed. But don't let that deter you. Coming off the addiction to speed can be a bit of a process. But the Spirit of truth will help you in digging out your well for Him to fill up.

He leads me beside the still waters. He restores my soul.
(Psalm 23:2–3)

If anyone had the right to choose to live out of ambition to fulfill the path of destiny, it was Jesus. Knowing He only had three years to fulfill his destiny on earth, to train up the twelve apostles and the other followers who traveled with Him, preach the kingdom, heal the sick, drive out demons, and everything else, Jesus certainly could have let his internal ambition to "work the work" rule his days and nights. But He deemed it necessary to go and be still in the presence of His Father, to restore and revitalize with the Holy Spirit. Jesus was showing and revealing the totality of a life of destiny. Half of the equation is private. Destiny lives and breathes in this intimate communion with God, relating an inner vitality, a moving and spiritual fire. This is the place where the Holy Spirit has complete control of the reins to direct our ambitions.

Experience is important, but we must "lie down in green pastures" to digest and develop what God is speaking to our hearts, so when we run, we have something real to run with.

DESTINY LIVES AND BREATHES IN THIS INTIMATE COMMUNION WITH GOD.

The Story of the Two Runners

In the eighteenth chapter of the second book of Samuel is a story that gives great imagery for this leadership scenario. King David awaits news of the outcome of a battle and the well-being of his son, Absalom. Joab, the captain of David's army, presided over the battle, and had to send word to David that while his army had emerged victorious, the King's son had been killed.

Before Joab could give directions to his men, a runner by the name of Ahimaaz, which means "Brother of Anger," asked Joab to let him run and bear the news of the army's victory to the king. Joab responded, *"You shall not take the news this day, for you shall take the news another day. But today you shall take no news, because the king's son is dead"* (2 Samuel 18:20). Then Joab turned to another runner, a Cushite, and said, *"Go, tell the king what you have seen"* (verse 21). The runner bowed to the captain and ran off.

But still Ahimaaz could not contain himself. Wanting so badly to be the one to run and to run now, he persisted and again asked Joab to let him run to the king. The captain then asked him, in essence, how he would run when he was not prepared or ready. Ahimaaz persisted, wanting to run. Joab, more than likely exhausted from battle, finally relented and simply tells him, "Run."

At this point in the story, we begin to get a glimpse of the crisis in this runner. His ambition is running him headlong into a situation where his true self is about to be revealed.

Although he had a late start, Ahimaaz's ambition fueled him to overtake the Cushite and he reached King David first. Ahimaaz called out to the king, "All is well!" Then he fell down in front of David and said his men were victorious in battle. King David made no comment on this news, instead asking the runner what was most pressing on his heart: was his son Absalom safe?

This was Ahimaaz's defining moment. His driving ambition and natural gift for running had projected him into this place, but his unprepared character would soon destroy this moment and reveal his immaturity. Unable to handle the idea of delivering the terrible news to the king that his son was dead, Ahimaaz lied. *"I saw a huge ruckus just as Joab was sending me off, but I don't know what it was about."* (2 Samuel 18:29 MSG).

The king's reply put an end to the runner's ambition. *"And the king said, 'Turn aside and stand here.' So he turned aside and stood still"* (2 Samuel 18:30 ESV).

In one moment, this gifted runner lost all credibility. He was talented and even had a position in the army, but his ambition pushed him past where his character could sustain him. When the second runner arrived, he gave David a full report without bias, including the news of Absalom's death.

The reality is that potential is one thing, but as one minister once shared with me, "Potential is not all of it. It is the intentions of your ambitions that must originate from the Father and not of you. If your intentions are being generated by your own ambition, then your character is lacking and you will fail."

> ## IT SHOWS TRUE CHARACTER TO SURRENDER YOUR INTENTIONS UPON THE ALTAR BEFORE GOD.

It shows true character to surrender your intentions upon the altar before God and ask Him for His intentions so those are the ones you are running with. That character will carry you through. We have to realize it is not solely the possibilities of your potential that matter most but the possibilities and development of your character. You must have both to achieve your divine destiny. True character is forged in places that originate in the secret place with God Almighty, where He has a firm grip on the reins of our heart so ambition does not drive us and attempt to take over.

As I watch my peers take their place as leaders in our generation and a new generation of future leaders arising behind us, it seems there are two groups emerging. One group includes those who are maintaining the status quo. They have learned the skills of working with and managing people and have learned how to gather, satisfy, and keep the masses.

The other group includes leaders who are radiating with something they have caught by divine impartation from places where there is a true, God-breathed spiritual culture. More importantly, they carry the flame of inspiration from their own closed off contemplation with the Holy Spirit.

We Need Spiritual Leaders

To be simply one or the other isn't the goal of any leader. The leaders of today and tomorrow should be those with skill and understanding so they can effectively reach people from every walk of life. They should be aware of the problems of our day and actively be a part and a source of the answers. But we also must be specialists in the realm of the Spirit and interpreters of the divine wisdom of God. We must be able to lead beside still waters because we ourselves have allowed Him to lead us by still waters. This is what we are called to do as believers. This must be developed in leaders.

The Word of God makes it known quite clearly that we are not to be ignorant of spiritual things. (See 1 Corinthians 12:1.)

You can be ignorant of something because of a lack of knowledge, meaning you simply do not know. Or you can be ignorant of something because you chose to ignore it. Either way, it leaves us coming up short.

We need to be aware of spiritual things because destiny originates in the realm of the Spirit. We must take time to know, understand, and recognize all that awaits us in the presence of God.

> "At any rate, when my laboratory has answered its last question and all other sciences have added their results to the pile, the real mystery of life has not yet been even touched."
> —Harry Emerson Fosdick[11]

The call to us is to be free from the need for speed, to match our pace to His, both internally and in our pursuits, to make sure our generation and the ones to come are not ignorant of spiritual things but participating in His divine realm.

> *For it is in closest union with Him that we live and move and have our being.* (Acts 17:28 WEY)

11. Harry Emerson Fosdick, "Science and Mystery," *Atlantic Monthly*, Vol. CXII (Cambridge, MA: Riverside Press, 1913)

Questions to Reflect on:

Why should we be concerned about how much information we receive each day and how fast it comes?

_____

_____

_____

_____

_____

_____

_____

_____

How can you know whether your ambition is pulling you away from your calling?

_____

_____

_____

_____

_____

_____

_____

_____

If you are in a situation where someone insists on acting wrongly or too hastily, what do you do?

_____

_____

_____

_____

_____

_____

_____

_____

_____

What are some ways you can discover your true character?

_____

_____

_____

_____

_____

_____

_____

_____

_____

_____

_____

CHAPTER 9

PRESSING THROUGH

Some people are natural born fighters. They seemingly just know how to push by nature. My mother is one of those people. She has never encountered a problem she couldn't find an answer to, or an obstacle she couldn't find a way around or, most times, blaze a trail straight through! Most people who know her would call her a natural overcomer. Maybe that's because she had to fight almost from birth.

My mother was diagnosed with leukemia when she was eighteen months old and the doctors gave her just days to live. But despite the odds against her, she pulled through and became free of this cancer. She has faced overwhelming circumstances in life and I watch people gravitate to her because she is the consummate fixer. If you don't want to hear a solution to your situation, then don't tell it to her because that is exactly what you're going to get coming back at you!

As her daughter, I have had a front row seat to her life and have watched my mother overcome. I understand it has had a great deal to do with how she thinks. She presses through because her internal posture is, "I know there has to be a way and I am not going to be pushed back." She also gets results as a woman of faith. She is thoroughly convinced of God's good intentions and His power to bring them to pass. I hope that in some way,

I have inherited this overcoming quality from her because I recognize it is exactly what it takes to live a life of destiny.

Thankfully, even though we were not all born able to meet any challenge, this ability was given to us when we became born again and gave our lives to Jesus Christ. The Word declares we are *"more than conquerors"* through Jesus Christ. (See Romans 8:37.) The DNA of champions was grafted into each of us when we made Jesus the Lord of our lives and He took His place on the throne of our hearts. His overcoming is our overcoming. And the Greater One who lives in us surges through us when opposition comes. He equips us to arise and press back.

> ## THE DNA OF CHAMPIONS WAS GRAFTED INTO US WHEN WE MADE JESUS THE LORD OF OUR LIVES.

Destiny Is Not Effortless

This is essential because the single greatest misconception about destiny is that it is effortless. Some think that because it is divine, how it will happen is a sovereign act of God and we have nothing to do with it. They believe the Will of God for your life just drops on you suddenly and you just have to wait for it to happen. They may say, "Well, if it is meant to be, then it will be, because after all, God is in control." We have all heard this phrase tossed around, a blanket statement covering possibility. But nothing could be further from the truth.

I think some people love to grab on to this version of destiny because it frees them from all responsibility. Of course, there is an overlaying element of God's grace that enables us to fulfill His will, but His grace is there for precisely that purpose: to enable you to press through all that you will face and all that most assuredly will oppose you on the path of destiny so you can overcome. Supernatural overcoming is a collaboration between God and man. The Bible is full of stories of overcoming and in each one, you see God's part and man's part.

Our destiny, our calling, follows a designated path by Father God. But it is not a given. When things press against you, you must act through

Christ who is in you and press back! If you don't, you will get pushed back instead of moving ahead.

THE ENEMY OF YOUR SOUL LOOKS FOR WAYS TO PUSH BACK AT YOU.

Opposition persists long enough to find out if you can be moved. If there is a type of pressure that causes you to relent, it will be used against you. The enemy of your soul looks for ways to push back at you. Financial pressure that causes you to cave in. The pressure of time, of feeling things are not happening when you think they should. Vocal pressure from critics, peers, and family and their opinions about your life. Appearance pressure—how you measure up in the eyes of society. If any of these things have a hold on you, it can press you into doing some strange things that can waltz you right off the path of your destiny.

But Paul, who knew something about personalized opposition coming against him, wrote about this scenario and we should keep his words on the tip of our tongues: *"None of these things move me"* (Acts 20:24 KJV). They may move other people, but they don't move me. Isn't it amazing how simple true wisdom really is?

Paul surely recognized what was happening to him and knew he had to make a decision: allow himself to be pushed back or press through. And with his words, he made his decision and took his stance of faith to believe.

Pressing through is a life-long occurrence. Now don't get me wrong, the life of the believer is meant for victory. The kingdom of God is made up of righteousness, peace, and joy. Some people take the posture of suffering and "warring" through life. I don't believe this is the destined path of a believer in Christ. And yet we have to recognize that we will face opposition confronting our peace, joy, and place of rightness in God. The pressing through or being pushed back is determined by what is inside you and what you are ready to act on.

"Leaders press through from the inside out."
—author Stephen Mansfield

I believe most people get lost in the press because they bend to the stress.

When the pressure comes, what's on the inside is not enough to sustain the weight of the moment. Pressure and stress reveal the weaknesses and expose the frailties. To press through, you need something solid within you. It's a common denominator in life.

Stress Brings Out True Colors

I had a friend who was dating someone for about four or five months. She was convinced he was almost perfect and he was surely the one for her. She talked about how patient, kind, and spiritual he was. How he carried himself as such a godly man during the time she had known him. But then they attended an important event where things didn't go his way. He began to stress out. All of a sudden—at least it seemed sudden to her—a totally different person emerged. He was self-centered and short-tempered. He began to blame her and point out all she had done wrong, even things that were out of her control, simply because things did not go the way he wanted. When other people whom he wanted to impress approached them, he changed into another person. He was so caught up in the charade, he acted as though he had no idea she was even there. He left her behind till the end of the night.

At first, my friend couldn't figure out what had changed in him so fast. Of course, he hadn't changed; he had been that way all along. When pressure came, stress revealed the fractures in his character. Thankfully, my friend found out early in this relationship.

None of us have reached perfection and we all have areas where we are growing as individuals. But grow we must! We need to be prepared to press through and refuse to be deformed by life's circumstances. In today's culture, people are too ready to give up. Quitting your job used to be a big deal but not anymore. Commitment doesn't mean much or hold much value because there is a way to quit just about anything. And let's face it: pressing through is tough. It takes effort. There is a reason it is called pressing through and not gliding through or sliding through. It has to come from something on the inside of us, from cultivating an inner life in relationship with God.

You and I can set ourselves up for success by making choices that direct our emotional and mental life in a positive way. No one else can do this for us. This is the effort of pressing through long before the push comes.

Speak from the High Road

Watching our words and what we speak about other people is a big part of our inner strength. Communication, good or bad, can strengthen or weaken you because your heart believes what it hears you speak. The challenge is to consistently speak from the high road. Anybody can gossip or give their opinion without consideration or concern for others. Anybody can polarize a situation, leaving room for only good guys and bad guys. But that is rarely the case. People can mishandle things but that doesn't make them evil. And in the end, saying anything to hurt others just weakens us.

> YOUR HEART BELIEVES WHAT IT HEARS YOU SPEAK.

On the other hand, communicating from a high road of believing the best—and remembering no one is at their best all the time and everyone can occasionally get things wrong—will add to your inner strength. Taking the place of grace when we communicate and speaking truth from this position is a noble thing and a strengthening way to interact. Just being conscious of relegating our emotion-filled opinion-sharing for the mere sake of saving strength sets you apart from the pack. So we press through in how we live, relate, and speak. When pressure comes, we are ready to press through and get to our destined places.

People who are good at pressing through didn't get there overnight. Learning to overcome helps you to become all that God put in you to be. Each time you decide to rise up and press through brings a new development of Christ in you. A long-time, dedicated, and seasoned ministry couple I have had the pleasure of knowing for many years once told me, "The way to truly get to know someone is to walk with them while they are having to overcome. Then you will see what is on the inside of them." Their wisdom has proven to be true time and time again. We can all attempt to personify what we think we are supposed to be, but who we really are is revealed when the pressure is on. Things are forged in you in times of pressing through. You are branded, in a way, by a strength that comes from not quitting and you are better for it.

Pressing Through Can Build Bonds

Pressing through with another person can be a bonding experience. It's what real relationships are made of, no matter what kind of relationship that may be. You know what is in one another. You realize, "You went through that with me and together, we experienced the tough parts and the breakthrough." It's not so much about how you do it; it's that you didn't leave. You were there. That sense of credibility and trust can stretch for years into some powerful, key relationships.

The effort of pressing through comes not in the heat of the moment but by having an inner life you have developed over time, where substance is added and a strengthening takes place. You develop an inner life through time spent with God, by reading His Word and spending quiet times before the Lord while you envision your life and your future. You also develop an inner life by spending time with people who challenge you and strengthen you as a person.

If you are totally focused on your output and never take any time to have something put in you so you can grow, you are setting yourself up for failure when pressure and stress come knocking at your door. Your character must be strengthened so you don't cave in. We need principles to sustain us and give us standards to hold so when faced with adversity, we can press through.

I have never been much of a fiction reader outside of some of the classics, but I do love to read biographies, especially of people who have overcome and lived lives of destiny. Their stories intrigue and inspire me. I also learn from the principles that enabled them to press through. Many times, I have adapted their principles as my own and it has added a great deal of strength to me. Sometimes, just seeing someone living from a higher standard or greater principles is the launch pad you need to come up to a new level yourself.

I once heard a story about a Christian businessman who owned a retail store many years ago in London. Inspired by a famous preacher whose crusade he had attended, he pinned the preacher's photo on a bulletin board in his back office. Every time a customer with a bad attitude pushed him to his limits and he wanted to lose his temper, or he was tempted to cut corners or cheat his suppliers, he would slip back into his office and look at that preacher's picture. To him, the preacher embodied the love of God and a man of excellence. When the businessman looked at the preacher's face, it inspired him to rise to that standard and put a strength in him to do what was right when he was tempted to do otherwise. But after months of doing this, he no longer needed to run back and look at that picture because those principles were now inside him and he shared the preacher's standard of excellence.

One of the biographies I have read is about John G. Lake, a godly man who changed nations. Lake lived by a set of eight personal principles that he determined would guide his life. These defined the kind of person he was going to be and served as the standards by which he lived his life. They are powerful and inspiring. They shine a light on why the power of God worked through Lake in such dynamic ways.

For the sake of modern day vocabulary, I will give you a summarized version of Lake's personal principles.

Personal Principle 1

Everything I possess I will not consider as my own but belonging to my Heavenly Father, and shall be held in trust by me to be used and directed by the Holy Spirit.

Personal Principle 2

I will carry a compassion for the lost. I will stay ready to cooperate with God in leading people to Christ.

Personal Principle 3

I will be a person of prayer. I will be sensitive to seasons of specific prayer and fasting.

Personal Principle 4

I will value living a clean, moral life as more necessary than my own happiness and not let myself be bribed or coerced into any unrighteous action for any reason.

Personal Principle 5

I will be a person of mercy and forgive those who have done me wrong.

Personal Principle 6

I will not allow any impure thoughts to linger in my mind. I will regard my procreative organs as sacred and holy and never use them for any purpose other than that which God created them for. I will regard marriage as sacred and always guard my actions in the presence of the opposite sex.

Personal Principle 7

I will always strive to be a peacemaker, avoiding pointless arguments. I will not try to force anyone to my point of view. If I should offend anyone knowingly, I will immediately apologize. I will not share bad reports about any person or repeat things that I am not certain of being true. I will not contribute to strife.

Personal Principle 8

I will not become discouraged or complain because of the high standards of life mentioned above. I gladly give my life rather than depart from these principles because I know I have a great reward in Heaven.

Closing

My goal will be to make the above principles the ideal of all the world and give my life and energy to see mankind get the power from God to practice them.

Principles like these inspire us all to press through no matter what we are facing.

Instead of cringing when opportunities to press through come up, look at the value that is about to be added to your life if you just don't give up. You have made it this far. Look at all you have pressed through to get to the point you are right now. Are you going to let the same old pressure and stress talk you out of your place now? Remember, you are not of those who draw back—you are of those who overcome. Listen to what the Word of God says about you:

> But we are not people who shrink back and perish, but are among those who believe and gain possession of their souls. (Hebrews 10:39 WEY)

> [You] shall fear no more, nor be dismayed, nor shall [you] be lacking, says the Lord. (Jeremiah 23:4)

> But as many as received Him, to them He gave the right to become children of God, to those who believe in His name: who were born, not of blood, nor of the will of the flesh, nor of the will of man, but of God. (John 1:12–13)

There is no quit in God so there should be no quit in you. Circumstances may make you think you should quit. Your emotions can make you feel like quitting. But during those moments, you have to stop what you're doing and take time to receive His grace, which has already been given to you for the very moment you are in. He has an unending supply of love and help to meet your every need. It is worth each place of effort and press when you realize that one day, you are inevitably going to take notice of where you are and you will either say, "I quit" or "I overcame."

Questions to Reflect on:

What are some misconceptions you have held about destiny?

Think of any obstacles keeping you from your destiny. How can you overcome them?

What should you do when under pressure or stress?

_____

_____

_____

_____

_____

_____

_____

_____

_____

_____

Why is it important to always speak in a positive way?

_____

_____

_____

_____

_____

_____

_____

_____

_____

_____

_____

CHAPTER 10

DOORS OF DESTINY

I start most days with a prayer to God that usually sounds something like this:

> "God, whatever you want, speak to my heart, for this day, I am open to hear it. I ask You to invade the privacy of my heart and, if necessary, I give You permission to rearrange the landscape of my life to put me in position for whatever You have for this time I am in right now. And Lord, I will be quick to obey. I declare over my day that I am prepared, equipped fully, supplied and ready, and I thank You for it. Holy Spirit, have Your way through me, in Jesus's name. Amen."

Do you ever get stuck on a word that just seems to float up in your thoughts at random times and you don't know why? I can't be the only person who is up late at night googling random words just to see what they mean. After a while, if you're like me, you start paying a little more attention to words and asking God what a certain word is all about. Then God starts talking to you about it and explains why it's coming up in you right now.

For the past few months, I have been having this experience. God often speaks to me in this way. The word coming up in my heart repeatedly is

DOORS. The more I have prayed about it and talked to God about it, the more He has expanded my understanding. He is talking to me about new doors and open doors. They are doors that I believe He wants us to be aware of and awake to the realization that they are coming.

DOORS REPRESENT THE OPPORTUNITY OF SOMETHING NEW.

Doors are important in life. Of course, they are symbolic in that they represent the opportunity of something new. How many times have we heard people say, "Is there any way that you could just get me in the door?" Or, "My door is always open." Or, "If God shuts one door, He opens another." A door is an entrance into a place of brand new possibilities.

It's essential then that we understand how doors work. When God gives us an opportunity, we want to handle it well. You could be standing in front of a door of opportunity, but if you don't handle it correctly, even though the opportunity was meant to produce something for you, you could miss out on its benefits. I have been there myself and I quickly learned it's not something I care to repeat.

Let's look first at doors of destiny. Revelation 3:8 says, *"I have set before you an open door, and no one can shut it."*

God sets doors of destiny before us. I believe there are specific doors attached to the blueprint and the destiny God designed for our lives, but how we approach those doors greatly determines the outcome. We can approach doors of destiny with either apprehension or expectation. Our approach makes all the difference.

Your Approach Determines Your Outcome

For example, take someone who is going for a job interview for a management position. This person may not have worked as a manager, but along comes this new opportunity through this interview. They can approach this door of destiny with apprehension or expectation.

They can be waiting for the interview thinking, "I'm not even going to get my hopes up. I've had three interviews for a management position in the past and three times, I've been denied." So on the inside, this person approaches this door with apprehension.

Of course, there's a problem with this approach. Apprehension affects the door of opportunity and how it turns out for you. Just even in the natural, we don't exude much confidence when we approach things apprehensively. It's safe to say that anyone who sees you probably won't notice anything very compelling or confident about you when you are apprehensive.

But when the job-seeker goes to that door with a sense of expectation, it shifts the whole dynamic and the outcome.

Now, it would be easier for us to believe that all doors, even doors of destiny, are all predetermined and sovereign acts of God. And unfortunately, there are people who believe this way and miss out on some really great divine opportunities for their lives. Haven't we all heard statements that people sometimes make like, "Well, you know, if it's meant to be, it will be." Or, "I am going to show up for the interview just as I am. It doesn't matter if my clothes are a little wrinkled. Who really cares?" Or, "I am just going to get through it and if it's God's will, it will happen for me."

I can tell you right now how that interview is going to go. If you don't understand how God works for us and with us, then you could be in danger of mishandling doors of destiny that God prepared for you. You see, doors of destiny require your key of faith so you can open them and step through.

DOORS OF DESTINY REQUIRE YOUR KEY OF FAITH.

I found out early on that even though I knew there was a divine calling for my life, it was still going to require some things of me. The call came and it had to be answered. It was not a one-time answer but a day after day answer from my heart of faith. These doors of destiny that come all along the path of our lives demand some things of us.

In our current cultural climate, it seems the number one thief of people's destiny is their "wait and see" approach. Their destiny is laid out in front of them, but they've lost the key to that door or they are fumbling with it. They need the key of faith to believe, speak, and move forward.

Don't Look Back

If I were to judge every door of opportunity by my past history, I would not get to experience the fullness of the opportunities that each door held for me.

The kingdom of God works in its own way. In God's kingdom, the way you approach a new door has everything to do with what's on the other side, waiting for you. Yes, it is predesigned for you by God your Father, but it is not already chosen.

Human nature pulls us toward apprehension because most of us have experienced places of disappointment in the past. Painful memories tend to make us pull away from a new opportunity.

> ### PAINFUL MEMORIES TEND TO MAKE US PULL AWAY FROM A NEW OPPORTUNITY.

Have you ever been there? A new possibility arises and just when you start to get your hopes up, your mind begins to replay and rehearse an event from your past. Maybe a particular person didn't respond the way you thought they were going to. Or a job didn't go the way you expected. Maybe you made a choice and then the road took a turn you weren't anticipating. Or maybe your hopes have been deferred, leaving you in a place of feeling heartsick, so your response to a new door of opportunity is something like, "But God, in this particular area of my life, there has never been an open door. It has always been closed. So I am afraid to hope and believe it could be true."

Let God Be Your Co-Author

And so we come out of mulling over the past and our reasoning wants us to use it to judge this new door in front of us. But there is a powerful truth for us to grab on to that will bring freedom from past disappointments. Your history is only bound to repeat itself if that's what you are constantly looking at. If you let go of it and make a new approach, you and God can write a new history for you together.

God is saying, "I need you to not judge this door I have prepared for you by the past. I need you to let it go. My Word says to behold this new door and look ahead at all that is before you, not what is behind you."

You can't look simultaneously back at your past and the door in front of you. Double vision will make you double-minded. There's a reason why Jesus gave us a warning about glancing back when He simply said, *"Remember Lot's wife"* (Luke 17:32). In Genesis 19:17, the angel warned Lot and his family, *"Escape for your life! Do not look behind you...lest you be destroyed."* But Lot's wife didn't listen. She looked back and turned into a pillar of salt (verse 26). God was saying in essence, "There is nothing for you back there. Everything I have prepared for you is waiting ahead."

GOD DOESN'T CREATE IN YOUR PAST; HE CREATES IN YOUR FUTURE.

The past is the past. We shouldn't say, "It is what it is" but rather, "It is what it <u>was</u>." God doesn't create in your past; He creates in your future. The dynamic of your faith isn't working behind you either. It's purposed, equipped, and empowered to work in your today, your tomorrow, your next year, and the rest of your life. Your approach has everything to do with how this door is going to open for you. How you look at your destiny and the words you speak will determine what happens. You and I have an opportunity to either judge each new door of destiny by the former events and people of our lives or listen to the Word of God.

> *Do not remember the former things, Nor consider the things of old. Behold, I will do a new thing.* (Isaiah 43:18–19)

Walking through doors of destiny requires us to trust in God's goodness so we can take confident steps forward. After warning His disciples to remember what happened to Lot's wife, Jesus tells them, *"Whoever seeks to save his life will lose it, and whoever loses his life will preserve it"* (Luke 17:33).

Living apprehensively will not spare you or save you. Living with expectation, on the other hand, will position you for God's best. It takes a core belief in your heart that what God has prepared for you is even greater than what He got you through.

LIVING WITH EXPECTATION WILL POSITION YOU FOR GOD'S BEST.

Zacharias Didn't Trust His Open Door

Woven into the beautiful story in the first chapter of Luke about Mary being pregnant with Jesus is the story of Elizabeth, Mary's cousin, and her husband, Zacharias. An angel of God visited Zacharias when he was in the temple and told him that even though he and his wife were old, her womb would be opened and she would bear a son. Can you imagine, an angel appearing to you and telling you, "I am going to open a door that no man could open for you and you couldn't open for yourself. Even though natural time has passed you by, the Lord says, 'This is My time. I will make this happen and I am going to bring you a son.'" Even more wonderful, the angel told Zacharias, this son *"will be great in the sight of the Lord....He will also be filled with the Holy Spirit, even from his mother's womb. And he will turn many of the children of Israel to the Lord their God"* (Luke 1:15–16).

But Zacharias's response to this news came out of his past disappointments. He told the angel, *"How shall I know this? For I am an old man, and my wife is well advanced in years"* (verse 18). He was stuck in a place of judging what God could do by what he had been through, even in the amazing moment of His visitation. But something else was at work here and there was another party involved. The promise wasn't just to him but also to his wife, Elizabeth. And she believed.

Zacharias's bitterness and lack of trust could have messed up things for his wife, who had wanted a baby her whole life. He could also have ruined things for all mankind since his future son was John the Baptist, destined to be the door for announcing the Savior of the world.

There is such an important lesson here. We need to pause and recognize that our door of destiny leads to other doors as well, some of which are ready to be opened by others. God is trying to bring something through you to put you in a place where you can affect more, influence more, and do more to bless the people around you. We don't want to waste our time getting caught in the confusion of our own emotions and past disappointments when other people are waiting for us to come through the door!

In the story of Zacharias and Elizabeth, before he could oppose the plan of God any further with his words, God prevented Zacharias from speaking until John was born. Through the angel Gabriel, God basically told Zacharias, "Before you mess up what I am trying to do and what Elizabeth your wife is believing will come to pass, I am going to do you a favor and shut your mouth."

This tells us how important it is to speak positively about our doors of destiny. As long as we are in faith, no one else is going to affect what God has planned for us.

As you are reading this, let me stress what I know to be true: no man, woman, or opposing force can shut your divine doors of destiny. No accusation or weapon that is formed against you is going to prosper when you approach your destiny with expectation rather than apprehension. We can hear what the response of faith and expectation sounds like in Luke 1:38—"*Be it unto me according to thy word*" (KJV)—and again in verse 45, "*The word spoken to her from the Lord shall be fulfilled*" (WEY). Those are the responses of believing hearts rising up over what emotions would try to dictate to them to believe.

Your Destiny Depends on Your Faith

Your destiny is dependent on your faith. It is dependent on us remembering who we are in Christ and speaking faith-filled words about our doors before we even get to them. Lastly, it requires us to willingly move forward and go through the door.

The purpose or call upon your life is sort of like an umbrella covering your whole time on this earth. But over the course of your life, God will bring you through a series of assignments or doors of opportunity. When God begins to lead you to a new door, going through it is imperative for you in fulfilling your life's purpose.

Sometimes, these doors or assignments from God look nothing like the big picture we have in our hearts. Have you ever had God lead you to do something and you think, "God, this isn't what I imagined. It looks nothing like the dream I had"?

I can remember when I was getting ready to graduate from Bible college and I was just waiting to hear from God about what He wanted me to do. I was so passionate for God and so eager to fulfill my calling. You can't sit under that kind of powerful teaching with such a spirit of faith for three or four hours every day and not come out feeling like you are ready to explode. In my young ignorance and vitality, I was just waiting on God to lead me straight from Bible college directly into something epic! As graduation approached, I was looking and listening for my new door. My graduation was about three months away and I was in a service. Worship was going on and I heard the still, small voice of God in my heart. And He said, "Jen, you've been asking Me for direction on what's next." And I thought, "Yes! Finally! Here it is!" He said, "Are you willing?" And I said, "God, You know my heart. I am so willing."

And then God spoke to my heart, "I want you to go back home and I want you to serve in your local church. Whatever they need you to do, I want you to do it." I am sure all of the color drained from my face. I couldn't have been more shocked. Immediately, all of my anticipation was crushed. I thought, "What did I do to deserve this!? I know I skipped a few days of school here and there, God, but does the punishment really fit the crime?"

I started to make my case. "Lord, I am carrying something big in my heart and You are the One who put it there! And now what You are asking me to do doesn't look anything like any of it!" I was learning a brand new lesson in living a life of destiny. The door that God puts before you is the only way you're going to move forward in God's calling for your life. There are no short cuts.

THE DOOR THAT GOD PUTS BEFORE YOU IS THE ONLY WAY YOU'RE GOING TO MOVE FORWARD.

I also learned another valuable lesson. God will let you spend all the time you want being unwilling, merely staring at that door. But there is no alternative route. If you want to spend six months saying, "I don't like this door. I don't like the way it looks. I don't like what's on the other side. Nothing in me wants to go through it," that is up to you. It was a painful lesson to learn. I could spend all the time I wanted criticizing the door, but it wasn't going to change anything or get me anywhere.

Our destiny awaits on the other side of the door. There, waiting for us to say "yes" to that door of opportunity, are people who need us to open it and step through because we carry something they need.

The faster you and I become willing, obedient, and move on through, the faster we receive the grace for the assignment of our life, following the plan and purpose of God. Once you get busy doing whatever He has asked you to do with a good attitude, the faster you move on to whatever He has next!

We Are in a Season of Doors

God wants us to know and understand what He is doing in our lives and what time and season we're in. I believe we are in a season of doors—of "right doors" and "open doors"—waiting for us to come through. He will take us up and over any obstacles and no man can shut these doors. You and I have everything to do with what lies ahead. As long as we approach with faith, we know we are making the right approach and our way will be easy.

In the culture and time of the Israelites, evil was so rampant, it was literally crawling through their city streets. It wasn't safe to go out at night. Civilization has seen some bad times before ours. But the strategy of heaven for the people of God was to take the blood of a lamb and put it on their doorposts. Not on the roofs or the floors but the doorposts, the entrances into their homes.

Jesus, the Lamb of God, tells us, *"I am the door. If anyone enters by Me, he will be saved"* (John 10:9). If you asked Jesus into your heart and gave Him entrance there, then His blood is upon the door of your life. So stand in that place. When trouble comes along, it cannot harm you. It cannot change your door or alter your season. Trouble will look you in the eye and try to get you to flinch, but it can't come in.

When I hear God saying, "It's a time of open doors and new doors," this tells me I have to look ahead. I can't look behind. And it tells me there is a grace to equip me with a new kind of strength and a new kind of equipment. I cannot do this the way I used to. I need a fresh equipping from heaven and I believe it comes as I go through the door. When I step through it, I am not going to panic because I don't know what it looks like or exactly how it works. I'm not going to judge my history by my past. I am going to let God lead me and show me. I believe the Spirit of God is saying, "I have set before you an open door and it is a new season. It is a new transition."

We are coming through and the past is no more. In fact, it is covered in the blood of Christ. If God doesn't remember the past, why should we? Join me in faith:

> Father, I thank You for how You have positioned us even in a time when there is chaos and turbulence. Lord, we are not moved. These things do not shake us. We were made for these days. Lord, not only were we made for these days, but we don't look at the chaos and the turbulence but look for the door of hope in the midst of the trouble around us. Father, I speak and declare over every person reading this that we will approach these doors full of faith, full of expectation. Lord, we make a decision today to cast off the former things. We cast off those places of doubt that would cause us to be apprehensive about what is before us. We lay aside the past because our eyes are looking for the things ahead. We speak and declare over these doors that You have orchestrated for us, which demand something of us. And we say that we answer the demand at hand with our trust and confidence in You. We believe You and take You at Your Word. Our trust is in the performance of Your Word. Lord, You said that faithful is He who has begun a good work in us and Lord, You are faithful to finish it. We thank You, God, that You are the author and finisher of our faith. Lord, we make a declaration that our eyes are fixed on what's ahead. We declare that we are a people who were made for latter days of glory, latter days of grace, latter days where we stand in great positions of authority. Father, we run our race with boldness. And we thank You for it.

You may be reading this and thinking, "I have been trusting and believing God, but I have sort of done it with one hand behind my back. I have done it apprehensively. My heart has risen up to believe, but there has been a piece of me that has said, Well, I hope it happens this time, but it didn't happen before."

I believe the Spirit of God is saying, "Release every trace of apprehension. Release every trace of 'what if,' 'but the last time,' and 'it wasn't that way before.'" God is saying, "Just let that go." Release yourself to be who God made you to be. Let the Spirit of faith and the overcomer rise up in you, so you step out in faith to believe God's promise of destiny for you. Speak to those things as the Bible tells us to—to the end from the beginning.

Father, we let all of the past go and we receive the Spirit of an overcomer. Be it unto me as You have spoken. My past will not dictate my future. I will not judge my present nor the road ahead by my past, Lord. We declare that You do a new thing and great things are ahead. We fix our eyes upon that and we thank You for it, Father. In Jesus's name. Amen.

Questions to Reflect on:

What doors of destiny are opening up for you?

_____

_____

_____

_____

_____

_____

_____

_____

_____

_____

Why should we "remember Lot's wife?"

_____

_____

_____

_____

_____

_____

_____

_____

_____

_____

_____

Where does the dynamic of your faith work?

How should you speak about your doors of destiny?

CHAPTER 11

THE PROCESS

"I only went out for a walk, and finally concluded to stay out till sundown, for going out, I found, was really going in."—John Muir

Sometimes, what God is doing in you has nothing to do with what you are actually doing. Instead, it's about what He is forming in you through what you are doing. You have to realize early in your life of destiny that potential requires a process to transform into power. Potential wants to be realized, but it needs a push. Sadly, it is typically during this process that most potential is forfeited, so the transformation never fully takes place.

In my own life, what has always beckoned me onward to take risks is the desire to see the possibilities of the potential that God placed within me become something useful and truly impactful in people's lives and in the world. Why else would I be here if not to effect change and make things better? If God wants to do it and He wants to use me, I cannot rest until I know I have reached for it. All I can do is reach, reach with faith, and take steps on that faith. Ultimately, God has to do it, but I have to reach. I have to see what can be within the realm of His will, leading me onward.

The compulsion to reach is not to test the boundaries of my own potential. That would be self-focused, self-absorbed ambition without purpose.

That does not interest me. The drive to do "your best," without considering God's plans for you, is destructive. Instead, I want to take every opportunity to stand firmly in the middle of what God has planned for me, for His kingdom to find shape through me.

> ## THE DRIVE TO DO "YOUR BEST," WITHOUT CONSIDERING GOD'S PLANS FOR YOU, IS DESTRUCTIVE.

I believe this is part of the DNA of all of us who are called. It was in Daniel when he was inspired to write from the depths of his heart, *"The people who know their God shall be strong, and carry out great exploits"* (Daniel 11:32). I feel that same beckoning in his words. You no doubt sense it in your own heart.

All of Us Can Help to Build the Kingdom

The idea of kingdom plans, concepts, ways of living, and building—yes! That is very enticing to me. That is what I will spend my life doing. In big ways and small ways, no matter whether something takes place quietly or amid notoriety, all are invitations to collaborate with God to change many lives or just one. This is the purpose for which each of us finds ourselves at this particular time in history.

Does this sound too grandiose? Let me show you why this is the truth and the only way to truly and fully live. The entire premise is laid out in the book of Isaiah.

> *Everyone who is called by My name, Whom I have created for My glory; I have formed him, yes, I have made him.*   (Isaiah 43:7)

Reading this verse, God makes known four powerful truths about us. He shows us that He is exact and particular in how He designed us. A process is involved.

1. *Called*
2. *Created*
3. *Formed*
4. *Made*

Now before we go any further, there is something you need to know about God if you don't know it already. God is never redundant. He is the ultimate genius, and He does not repeat Himself. He is exact and purposeful in everything He says and does. So there are things we need to understand when He says, "I called you. I created you. I formed you. I made you." At first glance, we could conclude He's telling us the same thing four times. But each word is separate and stands alone—and all of it points to something incredible that is going on in your life right now. Let's take a look at all that goes into the calling, creating, forming, and making of the person who is you.

CALLED

To be called out. To call forth. To invite. To name and proclaim. To publish, read, and say.

God sired you. He fathered you and called you forth from obscurity and into exact design. He fathered you in purpose—on purpose and for a purpose. He didn't keep that purpose to Himself. He purposed you for influence and function. He proclaimed it and published it. It is recorded in heaven that your purpose may have its authorized place to function on earth. In the grand scheme of eternity, it's being woven through every generation.

God wrote your purpose before you were born. He knew then the plans He had for you.

This took place before your creation, not the other way around. You did not first exist in physical form, then receive a purpose from God. No, in answer to a need, God contrived the idea of you and then audibly called you forth. He did this by calling you, audibly naming the purpose of you. He proclaimed, published, and spoke it. After this, your creation, your physical form, began to take place.

CREATED

There are three Hebrew words that refer to God's creating activity. The first one, *asah*, is used to describe when God makes something from something else He has already made, using something preexistent. The second word, *bara*, is used to describe when God makes something that has never existed, not using anything old—something brand new.

The second word describes when God made you. He made you from something that has never existed. You are organic. You are singular. When God created you, He made something brand new.

The word create also means to choose, to select. So what did God chose and select from to make you? There can be only one answer: from Himself. He is the only non-created One. We came from Him, quite literally. In purpose, in design, in Spirit. From and of Himself, the non-created One, God made you.

Only God can create in this way. This power is exclusively His. Romans 4:17 shines a spotlight on this exclusive ability, saying God *"gives life to the dead and calls those things which do not exist as though they did."*

You and I can create and make things, but we need materials. We cannot create without using something that already exists in some form. God stands alone in this power and ability to create something totally original. Even in the realm of the spirit, in the supernatural, anything not originating from God is only a cheap copy or an attempted replica of something God has made.

The third Hebrew word used in reference to God's full process of creating us, *yatsar*, is right there in Isaiah:

> Everyone who is called by My name, Whom I have created for My glory; I have **formed** him, yes, I have made him.   (Isaiah 43:7)

FORMED

The verb "form" can mean many actions, including to mold, shape, compose, develop in the mind, and fashion. Now I know I probably have the attention of some fashion-forward people right now, so let's take a look at God, the fashion designer.

To fashion means to give a particular shape or form to something, usually for a particular purpose. For us, this means that God has thought of us in a special way for a particular purpose, just like a fashion designer would take a piece of fabric to create an evening gown, a raincoat, or a pair of jeans.

This is key to anyone who desires to live a life of destiny and fulfill their divine calling. It is a very big deal and most people miss it.

Here's why: in God's mind, His creation is not completed until it has been formed. If you look at this with me for a moment, I believe this is going to help you to understand what God is doing in your life right now in a totally new way. Let's go back to the beginning, the story of creation.

In the beginning God created the heaven and the earth. And the earth was without form, and void; and darkness was upon the face of the deep. And the Spirit of God moved upon the face of the waters.
(Genesis 1:1–2)

No specific time period is given for this. It very likely took some time between the "creating" and the "forming." Although the calling forth of the earth had taken place and the creating of the mass (physical form) of the earth had occurred, the fashioning had not. The earth was *"without form... and darkness was upon the face* [the surface] *of the deep."*

God forms you and fashions you in the deep. The Hebrew word for deep refers to an immeasurable abyss. And the Spirit of God *"moved upon the face of the waters."*

When I think of God moving in such a fashion, I think of His Spirit hovering in a loving, protective way over His creation. Some people believe the Holy Spirit did not come to earth until the day of Pentecost, but this is incorrect. He was there right at the very beginning, forming and fashioning the earth itself. That's His artistry at work. This work of purposing you is the exclusive work of the Holy Spirit. This is why He calls you out into the deep waters of the Word and the person of Jesus, His presence.

For something of God to be truly and fully created, it must go through the process of being formed. That forming happens when the Spirit of God is moving upon the deep.

GOD IS FASHIONING YOU WITH HIS REVELATION WORDS FOR YOUR LIFE.

What is God doing in your life right now? He is forming you. He is fashioning you with His Word, His revelation words for your life that He is whispering to your spirit and branding upon your heart. All He is showing you and speaking to you is what is forming you. In reality, His words are carving out parts of you spiritually, emotionally, and mentally. In this, you are still being created until you are *made*.

God Is Always at Work

There is a tendency to assume this is happening mainly through spiritual events that you experience, but I believe this transformation takes shape in times that are less obvious. Our Christian culture sometimes falls victim to assuming that God is only at work when we are doing something overtly spiritual. But God cannot be limited in such a way.

I have encountered God at the strangest of times and have even found myself thinking, "God, what are you doing here!?" But He is everywhere and He is always speaking. He only needs us to discern and listen. God can speak to us when we take a long walk or go for a quiet drive. He can speak to us when we are working something over in our minds or hearts. God can speak to us when we choose to re-commit to commitments we've already made. This is when a forming and fashioning in us takes place.

> REMINISCING CAN SHOW YOU HOW SEEMINGLY INSIGNIFICANT THINGS WERE ACTUALLY IMPORTANT IN YOUR LIFE.

Reminiscing about your life can be a valuable thing. Recalling what you have pressed through and how you arrived at where you are now draws your attention to how God has been forming and fashioning you. You can also see how seemingly insignificant things were actually important in your life. To look back and recognize the forming and fashioning that God has been doing in you makes you realize how hands-on God really is in your life. This gives you a firm foundation of trust for the future.

Humanity wants to form and fashion itself, to be its own potter. But people who think this way are only fooling themselves. What we can do is yield to the process, let Him do the work, and go along for the journey.

The world changes things from the outside, but Jesus changes things from the inside out. His process can't be defined by the natural eye. It has to be discerned.

This is why the world has not seen the best of you yet. You have not reached the depths of who you were cut out and called out to be. You are still becoming. God the Father, God the Son, and God the Holy Spirit are still hovering over you, protectively and yet creatively working on the Father's original proclamation and statement He made of you in heaven. This is happening to you right now. His Spirit is hovering over the surface of your deep—the depths of who you are created to be.

Jesus, the Word made flesh, was present at the beginning of your becoming. He is still present in your forming and fashioning, leading to your being made.

MADE

There are so many synonyms for "made," such as accomplished, appointed, brought forth, invented, finished, formed, and shaped.

All things were made through Him, and without Him nothing was made that was made. (John 1:3)

All those things My hand has made, And all those things exist, says the Lord. (Isaiah 66:2)

But indeed, O man, who are you to reply against God? Will the thing formed say to him who formed it, "Why have you made me like this?" (Romans 9:20)

Because Jesus is the Word, knowing Him and hearing His voice will form you to fulfill what was uttered in the court of heaven when God declared you, proclaimed, and published you.

This is the full and complete process of fashioning and forming to produce the originally desired intention of the Creator. You are made in the image and likeness of God. This is who you are. We are made to discover all of the places He wrote about and planned for us, and arrive fashioned and prepared for those places. You and I do this by faith because of what Jesus did for us, making us new creatures in Him.

Being made is destiny realized and fulfilled. This is not just one event but a whole life lived from this process of creation, taking its full course at the hand of our Creator. Living for this destiny gives us a life worth living.

Questions to Reflect on:

How can you help to build up the kingdom of God?

Why do you think God specifically told the prophet Isaiah that He has called, created, formed, and made us?

When have you felt God at work in your life?

Looking back at your life now, what have you learned?

CHAPTER 12

KEEPERS OF THE MYSTERIES

I came across an interesting story about Harvard University recently. The school has an enduring prestige and impresses us as one of the top Ivy League schools in the United States. It was founded in 1636 with the intention of establishing a school to train Christian ministers. Ten years later, Harvard's "Rules and Precepts,"[12] were adopted. Here are two of the rules, with updated spelling:

> "2. Let every Student be plainly instructed, and earnestly pressed to consider well, the main end of his life and studies is, to know God and Jesus Christ which is eternal life (John 17:3) and therefore to lay Christ in the bottom, as the only foundation of all sound knowledge and Learning. And seeing the Lord only giveth wisdom, Let every one seriously set himself by prayer in secret to seek it of him (Prov. 2:3).
>
> 3. Every one shall so exercise himself in reading the Scriptures twice a day, that he shall be ready to give such an account of his proficiency therein, both in Theoretical observations of Language and Logic, and in practical and spiritual truths, as his Tutor shall require, according to his ability; seeing the entrance of the

---

12. http://www.hcs.harvard.edu/~gsascf/shield-and-veritas-history

word giveth light, it giveth understanding to the simple (Psalm 119:130)."

Pictured here are Harvard University's original seal, left, and its seal today.

The original motto, in Latin, was "Truth (Veritas) for Christ (Christo) and the Church (Ecclesiae)."

At some point in the school's history "Christ and the Church" were removed from the motto and the seal. The Harvard seal now simply says, "Truth." What was once a place of higher education founded on the Word of God, where being stewards and keepers of the mysteries of God was the basis for all understanding, now believes that truth stands on its own.

How can truth be found apart from God? God is the ultimate authority. It seems that ever since this shift in foundational truth occurred in our places of higher learning, the United States' original purpose has been under siege.

The Mystery of Destiny Pulls Us

Each one of us carries a desire to find the path that leads us out of the trivial and into the significant. We want to matter. And we are all moving toward that desire.

When I look at Jesus's path of destiny when He walked the earth, I watch Him lead people out of their busy environments and on to a quiet hillside to speak to them of His Father and their destiny. He revealed to them who He really was and who they really were. He talked to them about their lives and the purpose of their days. I think the mystery of who He was and the desire to look into the mystery of who they were, and what life was really about, compelled them to follow Him.

JESUS LAYS HOLD OF THE DIVINE WITHIN US AND HE WON'T LET GO.

Today, He is still doing the same thing! Jesus calls us by our dreams. He thrills us by each high aim that inspires us in this life and points out this great kingdom of His that is yet to be on the earth. He lays hold of the divine within us and He won't let go.

This kind of destiny life is meant for the lion-hearted who are armed by faith and branded with fire. It is meant for those who wear robes of righteousness, knowing who they are and Whose they are, for those who know they belong to something much bigger than any one person. They belong to the great innumerable company of the redeemed. The mystery and path of destiny is worn by the feet of generations. For me, part of the thrill is knowing that my feet now trod where they once walked—into the unknown.

As Anna Robertson Brown Lindsay put it:

"Arise and do what Jesus bids. Heaven is heaven because no one is unruly there, or idle, or lazy, or vicious, or morose. Each soul is at true and happy work. Each energy is absorbed; each hour is alive with interest, and there are no oppressive thoughts or ways. If each heart and soul responded to the call of Jesus, there would be a new heaven and a new earth...Each hand would be at its own work; each eye would be on its own task; each foot would be in the right path."

This deep-seated, unseen truth compels me to "build my life on the mystery of where (He) calls me."[13]

The unknown is outlined in intrigue and only the curious will venture out into it. This kind of curiosity is found in a courageous heart. In fact, the

---

13. Mosaic MSC, "Unknown," on *Unknown* (Essential Worship, 2017)

word "courage" comes from the old French word for "heart" or "innermost feelings."

The mystery of destiny compels us to get out of the boat of what we know and walk on the water toward the unknown. This takes courage. The things we know and the things we don't know we discover only as we go. The Spirit of God gives us glimpses to stimulate us to lift our eyes up to the Source of our help and take our place as keepers of the mysteries of God.

MERELY PEERING OFF INTO THE UNKNOWN WON'T BRING YOU INTO IT.

Some people walk right up to the edge of an uncertain future because their curiosity draws them there. However, just coming up to the edge and considering what could be is not enough. Merely peering off into the unknown won't bring you into it. If you're going to step into your divine destiny, you have to take steps forward and walk on in. Without this courage in your heart to step in where it's leading you, your destiny will remain vague and won't materialize.

Sometimes, we can find our day-to-day world so engrossing that we do not push out to explore the mystery that "passes all understanding." The sights and sounds of our current life distract us from the spiritual pull to a place unknown. We trade in our inner destiny DNA as an explorer and pioneer to become citizens of a land-locked life. We soon forget who we are and where we came from. We can get so good at learning how to control our environment that it gives us a false sense of confidence about our own power of self-improvement and a decreased sense of our dependency on Him.

It has been said that if you allow yourself to be dazzled by your own achievements or gifts, your sight will be clouded so you cannot see the true things of God. We have to watch that we don't overemphasize our giftings, our anointing, and intelligence. These are no substitute for God and His realm of mystery.

We Have Reached a Turning Point

Right now, in the body of Christ, we are at a turning point, a decisive place that is going to define the church for future generations. What we are *saying* is not as important as what we are actually *doing* and *not doing*. We are passing down to future generations who the body of Christ is in the modern world.

Lately, I've heard a concern echoed by Christian leaders around the world that we could be in danger of handing the next generation the wrong impression if we are not careful. I believe we need to evaluate what we are communicating, verbally and nonverbally, to take a look at what we are conveying by our actions regarding what's important and what isn't. As one minister put it, "We could be in danger of acting like some things are now taboo for Christians. It's not that we don't believe in their validity, it is just that they have become today's taboo in our gatherings."

Something is taboo when it's not mentioned, considered, or used. It could never be said that God the Father, God the Son, and God the Holy Spirit are not honored in our midst—but are they employed?

There is a felt desire among Christian leaders for the rising generations to grab hold of what really matters and make sure what is being passed down to them is their heritage of faith and the spiritual treasures of impartations that are rightfully theirs. The danger is that whole generations may grow up with gaping holes where inner spiritual deposits and graces should be residing. Up and coming generations of believers must be given glimpses of spiritual wonder into the things of God and hear the compelling call to "go further" into a deeper place of experiencing Him. They must know the necessity of hunger for God and the pursuit of Him. They need to understand that it is only the hungry who become carriers of those spiritual impartations that can change nations.

Tomorrow's Leaders Need to Know the Past

Not long ago, I was asked to speak at a Bible college in Texas. This school has been raising up ministers and missionaries for over four decades. During a break in my session, I talked with some of the younger students. I love to hear their stories of how God worked in miraculous ways so they could come to Bible college for training. You can see the passion in their eyes. They are so singularly focused on preparing for the life ahead.

As we were talking about what God was doing in the world, I mentioned something that a great man of God, Lester Frank Sumrall, once said. One student looked at me and asked, "Who is Lester Sumrall?" I couldn't believe it. I said, "You don't know who Lester Sumrall is?" They had no idea. I said, "He was the guy who was mentored by Smith Wigglesworth!" Another student asked, "Smith who? That name kind of sounds familiar..."

I was in shock. I said, "Smith Wigglesworth! You don't know who Smith Wiggleworth is? He was the man who had fourteen people raised from the dead during the course of his life!" Now they were locked in; they wanted to know who this man was! I went on, "One time, he went with his pastor friend to a visitation for a man from his church who had died. While the pastor was busy consoling the family, Smith went in to the room where the man's body was laid out. He pulled the body up out of the casket, threw it up against the wall, and commanded him to live in the name of Jesus!"

CHRISTIANS HAVE BEEN WORKING THE SUPERNATURAL FOR CENTURIES.

The look on those students' faces was priceless! They had never heard this story and they were amazed. I said, "You guys, Harry Potter has nothing on us! Christians have been working the supernatural for centuries!" It made a great impression on me that day. Here were these young students training for the ministry and they had no idea of the kind of power that men of God who had gone before them had walked in, not that long ago.

This startling realization was cemented in me further a few months later when I was speaking at another Bible college, this time in Oklahoma. Again, after the class, I was talking with some students. They asked me about my years as a Bible school student and I shared some stories of that time. This group was serious about what they were training for and I was impressed by their hunger for information as they listened. As we continued to talk, they were full of questions. I had just returned from the nationwide women's conference that my team and I held in Grenada. Many of the students had followed the event through social media and they were intrigued. After a while, a few started to ask questions like, "So who made that happen for you?" "Who opened that door for you?" "How did you get to meet so and so?" and "How long did it take you to get to do that?" This was the moment when I realized, "They are beginning to lose sight of kingdom motive, which is why we do what we do."

I left with a newfound determination to ensure that the coming generations understand that ministry is not about being viewed by the masses. These coming generations are watching what we do and what we don't do. They are watching for what we deem important and what we deem inconsequential. Who we make room for and who we don't. We must get busy ensuring they are given the right impression because we are at a turning point. My heart is so stirred about what God is doing right now among every generation. We have a responsibility to pass down the realities of the mysteries of God. The generation rising is fueled with passion to run, but we cannot hand them all of the enhancements without giving them spiritual hardware first.

The Coming Generations Want God

It's a mistake to believe they aren't interested. Those I encounter want to be taken to the wells of their fathers so they know where to go and can drink for themselves. They long to see the supernatural and experience the impossible. In short, they want God. They don't desire a go-between. They want access to the realm of mystery for themselves. They want to go and explore all that God can reveal to them, One-on-one. And they also are determined to reach and change the world.

What if we allowed what we prioritize today in our ministries to leave the general impression that we are here to serve the good opinion of people? That it's okay to run things centered around what people prefer, rather than the works of the Holy Spirit? That gaining "likes" and being likable is our mission? That when it comes to affecting the world, we have assumed the work of seeing justice done through our own means? That becoming impatient with the unseen work that faith does, we have traded it in for displays of gravitas and personality? And in place of waging battles for our cities in prayer, we now look to demonstrations in the streets?

This just cannot become our subconscious culture.

There is so much that needs to change in our world, so much injustice that goes on every day. But the truth is, we do not see a call to social justice in the Word of God. We do, however, see a call to follow Jesus. And when that call is answered, the release of His kingdom takes shape and it meets every cry of social justice fully and completely in the form of Jesus our King.

WE HAVE TO BE CAREFUL TO NOT BECOME SELF-APPOINTED SOCIAL CRUSADERS IN PLACE OF OUR DESTINY.

We have to be careful to not become self-appointed social crusaders in place of our destiny, trading in the Holy Spirit for a humanistic spirit of righting wrongs in our own strength. This would be a lesser version of what God has prepared for us. It is self-directed and not God-appointed.

I am not anointed to change everything. I am anointed and appointed to what He tells me. This is where my power lies for good effect. It all hinges upon what He gives to me as I spend time with Him in His realm of mystery. That is when my destiny starts speaking. He speaks, then I speak. He shows me how to move, then I move. If I wind up on a platform, it is only to say what I have been anointed to say. If I wind up in the streets, it is because God has directed my feet there.

Only that which comes from divine guidance can change our world for the better. In this way, we are powerful because we have been given access to God's divine realm of mystery, where answers come to meet every need.

Our greatest job as leaders is not to win the hearts of the masses but to take them by the hand and walk them down the well-worn paths to meet with God for themselves. It is to teach them how to develop that inner place with Him, where they can stay in fellowship with Him and be close to Him.

The progressive spirit within this generation carries a healthy desire to see the God of their salvation alive and be an active part of it. They realize that merely looking modern does not have the power to transform a life, but God is transforming lives in new, fresh, and exciting ways. All of us together, leaders of every generation, are still here to be pioneers. There is so much truly beneficial information and knowledge available to us that can help us do things effectively in our churches, ministries, and organizations. If we want to reach people, we should take advantage of it.

But knowledge and reason have never initiated the great movements of life. They have helped to correct and direct them but have not supplied the initial spark. We must be wise enough to utilize modern methods, programs, polls, statistics, and popular opinion yet recognize their limitations. We must be bold enough to push beyond these.

We are runners in the same race with the men and women of God who have gone before us, saw a more excellent way, and with undimmed eyes of faith, saw the supernatural. We cannot be content without it. Each one of us desires the real, potent, influential, and convincing gospel that carries an irresistibility to it. This is the power propelling our advance today.

There is a mystery connected to all that God does. It is that mystery, the path of discovery, which has always compelled me to continue on. In the Word of God, Paul calls us *"stewards of the mysteries of God"* (1 Corinthians 4:1). It is the mystery of all that God is and what He does that stirs the deepest part of my heart today. And I would dare say I am not the only one.

When I stop and think about the seriousness of that charge, *"stewards of the mysteries of God,"* I realize again how much God has placed in our hands and entrusted us with. The word "steward" means an overseer, manager, governor, agent, or treasurer. This gives us a glimpse into God's thoughts about us based on the Word. We are truly co-heirs, co-laborers, and joint-heirs with our big brother, Jesus! This is a far cry from the frail, sin-focused notion, crippled by our own humanity, which some believers still tuck away in their minds about themselves.

We Must Focus on the Light

We are also not supposed to spend time considering prey-focused wolves or defenseless sheep. Our focus should not be on attacking evil or defending against it. Jesus showed us that the attraction of His goodness was the most superior strategy for overcoming evil. Darkness cannot be eradicated by a weapon but by turning on the light. When light enters a room, every shadow leaves. As forces of righteousness in the earth Jesus called us *"the light of the world"* (Matthew 5:14).

This makes us stewards of the mysteries of this life-changing kingdom of God.

God may give us charisma and gifting, but these are not our fuel supply and we can't go far with them alone. However, when we are full of God and spend time in His mysteries, He takes us to a limitless experience of real transformation. We cannot promise that everyone will see what we have seen. In God's realm of mystery, everyone has to adventure out for themselves. It's one thing to acknowledge the validity of the realm of the Spirit and another thing to be in working relationship with it. But God has given us access to that realm. As believers and keepers of the mysteries of God, it's our job to help people encounter what God has waiting for them.

Theologia Germanica, a manuscript published in 1516, pointed out:

"Now the created soul of man hath also two eyes. The one is the power of seeing into eternity, the other...of giving life and needful things to the body...But these two eyes of the soul of man cannot both perform their work at once; but if the soul shall see with the right eye into eternity, then the left eye must close itself and refrain from working, and be as though it were dead. For if the left eye be fulfilling its office toward outward things; that is, holding converse with time and the creatures; then must the right eye be hindered in its working; that is, in its contemplation. Therefore whosoever will have the one must let the other go; for 'no man can serve two masters.'"[14]

Spend Time in the Secret Place

To spend time in God's realm of mystery, we don't have to remove ourselves from our day to day life, but we do need to learn how to detach from it at times. And each time we do, we find a wealth of spiritual life that spills over into every part of us. It integrates our whole being. When a crisis occurs, we center ourselves in the realm of mystery to feel the Spirit of God backing us up. Time spent with God fills us up so we can live from the heart and have courage for everything that we face. Without those times, there is a great void in our lives.

Many people are yearning to live from the heart; their souls thirst to connect and feel. We who do know God are called to help them find and rediscover Him. He is the Source of living water without limits, ever ready

14. http://www.ntslibrary.com/PDF%20Books/Theologia%20Germanica.pdf

to quench thirsty souls. We were made to be with Him, to live in awe and joy, hope and wonder, excitement and adventure.

> **WE WERE MADE TO BE WITH HIM, TO LIVE IN AWE AND JOY, HOPE AND WONDER, EXCITEMENT AND ADVENTURE.**

Take time to discern the things that lie beyond the rational, beyond what your head can figure out, and beyond your natural experiences with their fleeting moments of happiness. You were made to feel alive! Spend time in the presence of God and in His realm of mystery. God wants to speak to you, but He wants to hear from you first and know that you are listening. Understanding that He is on your side at all times will give you the enthusiasm and zeal you need for life and your destiny.

> *Can anyone hide himself in secret places, so I shall not see him? says the* Lord. *Do I not fill heaven and earth?*   (Jeremiah 23:24)

God has so much He wants to share with you and a special calling just for you. Jesus says:

> *Ask, and it will be given to you; seek, and you will find; knock, and it will be opened to you. For everyone who asks receives, and he who seeks finds, and to him who knocks it will be opened.*   (Matthew 7:7–8)

Notice that He invites us to ask, seek, and knock—and He stands ready to answer us and open the door. He is waiting for you. What are you waiting for?

Questions to Reflect on:

Why is God so important when we try to discern the truth?

What thoughts come to mind when you think about past and future generations?

How are you a "steward of the mysteries of God"?

What have you learned about your destiny and calling?

ABOUT THE AUTHOR

Jen Tringale is an internationally known speaker, author, and strategist on awakening destiny. She is known for her integration of purpose, innovation, faith, and spirituality. Her messaging reaches across cultures and vocations to unlock the purpose and potential within individuals, organizations, cities, and nations.

Her reach includes a robust international speaking schedule, her books, *Your Defining Moment, When Time and Destiny Meet*, and *Calling, Understanding Your Purpose, Place and Position*, and a podcast that opened in iTunes' Top 40 charts with an audience of more than thirty thousand listeners in over fifty nations.

Her international influence includes meetings with heads of state, cabinet members, and U.S. Embassy and State Department representatives. In 2016, she hosted a history-making, nationwide women's conference in the nation of Grenada. It was the first of its kind, with thousands in attendance, including dignitaries and prominent leaders. After over twenty years of ministry, Jen is positioned as a leading voice in the current generation who communicates with clarity, boldness, and passion on divine destiny and bringing Jesus Christ into culture.

Her initiatives to equip and empower extend beyond the pulpit and pew into every arena of culture for influential shift. She has appeared on television networks such as TBN, TCT, and the Believers Voice of Victory Network, and has been featured in the *Word of Faith Magazine*.

Jen is a graduate of Rhema Bible College, and is originally from Florence, KY. She embraces both her southern roots and Italian heritage, and now resides in Nashville, TN.

———

If you've read this book and have additional questions or thoughts, I'd love to hear from you.

You can find me on:

+ Instagram @jentringale
+ Twitter @jentringale
+ Facebook @jentringale
+ YouTube: Jen Tringale

You can also email me at info@jentringale.com, listen to the Jen Tringale Podcast on SoundCloud, iTunes, and Google Play; and visit the website at jentringale.com.

Welcome to Our House!

We Have a Special Gift for You

It is our privilege and pleasure to share in your love of Christian books. We are committed to bringing you authors and books that feed, challenge, and enrich your faith.

To show our appreciation, we invite you to sign up to receive a specially selected **Reader Appreciation Gift**, with our compliments. Just go to the Web address at the bottom of this page.

God bless you as you seek a deeper walk with Him!

WE HAVE A GIFT FOR YOU. VISIT:

whpub.me/nonfictionthx

WHITAKER
HOUSE